Richard

W9-CDY-448

Summer 1982

THE INDIAN PRIEST
Father Philip B. Gordon
1885 - 1948

THE INDIAN PRIEST: FATHER PHILIP B. GORDON, 1885-1948, by Paula Delfeld. Copyright ©1977 by Franciscan Herald Press, 1434 West 51st Street, Chicago, Illinois 60609.

Library of Congress Cataloging in Publication Data:
Delfeld, Paula.
    The Indian priest, Father Philip B. Gordon, 1885-1948.
    1. Gordon, Philip B., 1885-1948. 2. Chippewa
Indians—Biography. 3. Catholic Church—Clergy—
Biography. 4. Clergy—United States—Biography.
I. Title.
E99.C6G643   282'.092'4 [B]   76-44869
ISBN 0-8199-0650-6

NIHIL OBSTAT:
    Mark P. Hegener O.F.M.
    Censor Deputatus

IMPRIMATUR:
    Msgr. Richard A. Rosemeyer, J.C.D.
    Vicar General, Archdiocese of Chicago

January 17, 1977

MADE IN THE UNITED STATES OF AMERICA

THE INDIAN PRIEST
Father Philip B. Gordon
1885 - 1948

by

PAULA DELFELD

FRANCISCAN HERALD PRESS
Chicago, Illinois 60609

FOREWORD

By Father Gordon's Best Friend, PAUL VILLAUME

~~~~~~

The Indian Priest IS THE LIFE-STORY OF A DEAR FRIEND OF
mine, a wonderful priest, a holy man, a proud American Indian,
and a good citizen.

Father Gordon deserves what Paula Delfeld has so carefully
researched and written. She writes gloriously of his pride in his
Indian heritage. She tells of his priestly qualities. He loved God
through his deep Catholicity; he loved the priesthood of the
Catholic Church. Most importantly she tells the reader about a
man who was loved by those who knew him well — as a
priest, a scholar, a raconteur, a leader in the fight for man's
dignity no matter what his origin.

He was a most important part of my life from 1925 to 1948,
age 10 to age 33. In the book he comes to life in a very real
sense.

In this short introduction I pay tribute to my dear friend and
to the lovely lady who has done her difficult job so well. Father
Gordon would have loved it. — P.V.

CONTENTS

INTRODUCTION

~~~~~~

AMONG THE NUMEROUS ARTICLES I HAVE HAD PUBLISHED, about 300, a subject occasionally emerges that seems to warrant more than just an article. Such was the case with the story of the first Indian priest, Father Philip Gordon.

For several years I had acted as chauffeur for an elderly couple, Mr. and Mrs. Orrin McGrath, to take them to their cottage at Minong, Wis., ten miles from Gordon, the birthplace of Father Gordon.

The McGraths, who now reside in North Fond du Lac, had lived in northern Wisconsin for many years and knew the country well. Orrin, better known as "Mac," had spent twenty-five years researching historical events in the area and has written a large volume of poetry about people, places, rivers, old trading posts, etc.

Among Mac's interests was the Gordon family. He showed me an "Outline for Biography of a Chippewa Indian Who Became a Catholic Priest," a 43-page booklet which apparently had been written with the intention of using it for writing an autobiography, with the help of Dan Wallace and Fred Holmes. No book was ever completed as far as I was able to ascertain. Apparently, they were all advanced in years and were unable to complete the project. Father Gordon had mentioned sending a manuscript to Dan Wallace but none has been found. He may have referred to the outline.

3

The more I heard about Father Gordon, the more interested I became. I wrote to the Wisconsin Historical Society to find out what they might have about him. It was very little, but they mentioned a column the priest had written for four years in the *Inter-County Leader,* published at Frederic, Wis.

I had heard of this newspaper, published in a small town in Polk County, from Bernice Abrahamzon, who is employed there. I wrote to her and she assured me that Father Gordon had indeed written a series of articles entitled, "History of St. Patrick's and Other Interesting Events." The only problem was that the series was not on microfilm but in bound copies, and they had no way of reproducing the articles.

Bernice quoted a few sentences and said there was a wealth of information. I was intrigued. I wondered why I had never heard of the Indian priest. I went to Frederic and photographed all the columns, written weekly for four years, and worked during my spare time the following winter, making prints of the film I had taken. It was not easy, but it was the beginning of two years of research, resulting in this book.

After considerable correspondence, research, travel, and interviews, I was nearing the end, but I was sadly lacking information about Father Gordon's later years. Almost all his contemporaries were dead. I found people here and there who were young during Father Gordon's time, and remembered him, but few who knew him intimately.

At some point I had checked the St. Paul directory for the name of Villaume, after seeing photos of Paul Villaume in the above-mentioned outline. I found a Paul Villaume in the directory, and assumed he would be a descendant. I knew Paul Villaume had named his son Philip Gordon after the priest but he might have had another son or a nephew.

I contacted Paul Villaume and was amazed to find he was the original. He was quite young when he traveled with the Indian priest. I went to St. Paul to interview him. He was extremely interested in my project and furnished much of the information for the later years of Father Gordon's life as well as some interesting photos.

In the book I hoped to show the development of an Indian boy who knew life on the reservation, but rose above discrimination, became educated and spent his life fighting for the cause of the Indians and for unity of religious and ethnic groups.

Father Gordon was ahead of his time in his attempt to combine two worlds, the Indian and the white, and the spiritual and the human.

CHAPTER
I
The Indian Priest Reminisces

~~~~~~

THE AGING INDIAN PRIEST SAT, AS HIS ANCESTORS HAD, BESIDE
the war drum. A stiff breeze whistled through the tops of the tall
pines, but beneath their sheltering branches, the eagle feathers
in his war bonnet were barely ruffled. Although the priest was a
Chippewa, the headdress he often wore was Sioux; he received
it while he was doing mission work in the western states.

Along the sandy river bank a campfire, adding its glow and
warmth to the cool June evening in the north woods, accentuated
the priest's Indian features and his ample figure. Around him
sat twenty St. Paul, Minn., Boy Scouts, eagerly waiting for the
proceedings to begin.

Friends of the scouts and the priest had gathered at the camp
the scouts called Neibel to witness the presentation of the Chippewa war drum and peace pipe to the troop by Reverend Philip
Gordon (Ti-Bish-Ko-Gi-Jik). The Calumet or peace pipe had
always been sacred to the Indians, and like the drum, its presentation was attended by strict ceremony.

Among the spectators was Luther Youngdahl, Minnesota's
governor and a friend of Father Gordon. He had invited the priest
to drum out a song.

For forty years the drum had been used for tribal ceremonies
and it was said that on a calm night it could be heard for ten

miles. But now the sound reverberated through the dense woods, one of the few stands of virgin timber remaining in the once heavily forested area.

Father Gordon began a slow beat. Scout Leader, Arthur Kingsbury, felt a tremor of apprehension for his friend, the priest from Centuria, a little village in Polk County, Wisconsin, close to the Minnesota border.

Faster and faster Father Gordan beat the drum, unmindful of his priestly garments. It was as though he could beat out the demon that was beginning to torment his body as his mind and spirit had been tortured through much of his life.

Philip Gordon's youth had been spent in the transition period between the fur trading years in the wilderness and the slaughter of the giant forests by the lumber industry. His life was torn between the free spirit of the Indian and the rigid rules of the Catholic Church of that time. But even after years of education and travel, his heart remained with the Indians. He often said, "I want to live and die among my people."

The priest began to chant an ancient tribal song to the accompaniment of the drum. For a few moments he was transported in memory to his childhood days and his somber garments became the colorful ceremonial robes of the Chippewa Indians. Tears came to his eyes as he lay down the beaters for the last time.

When Father Gordon had become the first American Indian in the United States to be ordained a priest in the Catholic Church, he ordered the war drum and peace pipe made so he could present them to Me-Sa-Bi, his childhood playmate.

Me-Sa-Bi had become the hereditary Medicine Chief at the Court d'Oreilles Reservation, the shaman of the Ottawa band of the Chippewa Confederation. The Indians believed the shaman had supernatural powers. He ranked above the chiefs and had more influence and greater prestige.

After the death of Me-Sa-Bi in the early 1940's, the Indian articles were returned to the priest. Father Gordon had always been a champion of scouting and wanted the Boy Scouts, who were interested in Indian lore, to have them.

Sixteen years after the presentation, the gifts were destined to be carried to one more chief, the Great White Father in Washington. On June 18, 1962, the centennial of the Indian Uprising in Minnesota, the Boy Scout Calumet Dancers from the Minnesota Council, presented the drum and peace pipe to President John F. Kennedy and repeated the legend.

As the echoes of the drum died away, Father Gordon returned to the parish house but he could not dismiss the nostalgic mood of the evening. His thoughts were back in the little village of Gordon where he was born on March 31, 1885. He was one of fourteen children of William Gordon and his Chippewa Indian wife, A-Te-Ge-Kwe (Woman Who Loves Gambling).

When Philip was born, Gordon, or Waiskamig in Chippewa tongue, was still not much more than a trading post and a mission of the Catholic Church, with a few Indian and white families. The village was named for Anton Gordon, Father Gordon's grandfather. He had Americanized his name from the French, Antoine Gaudin, when he built the log trading post at the place the Indians called Amick.

The mission was visited only a few times a year by Franciscan missionaries from Bayfield, Wis., about eighty miles away.

These dedicated missionaries journeyed through the wilderness to visit Indian villages and white settlements throughout northern Wisconsin. They suffered unbelievable hardships in establishing friaries and mission stations to serve the scattered settlements. In order to reach as many as possible, they divided the extensive area into four districts. The mission at Gordon was included in the St. Croix valley district, along with Yellow River, Yellow Lake, Mud Hen Lake, Orange, Trade River, and others.

In the beginning, the missionaries made the journey on foot with one or two Indian guides, as only an Indian could find the trails in the dense forests. Since the trip required six to eight weeks, provisions, blankets, and tents as well as the necessary articles for divine services, had to be carried. They struggled through mud and swamps in the rainy seasons and were often drenched to the skin without a change of clothing.

Northern Wisconsin's severe winters were another hardship they had to endure. The Indians taught them to make and use snowshoes which made winter travel somewhat easier. Even warm weather brought discomforts with swarms of mosquitoes emanating from the swamps and lush growth of vegetation. Later the missionaries made the trip on horseback or with a horse-drawn wagon or buggy.

During their visits, the missionaries celebrated the Mass, heard confessions, administered baptism and performed marriage ceremonies for those who were joined by Indian rites.

The first two Franciscan missionaries who had their headquarters at Bayfield were Fathers Casimir Vogt and John Gafron. Others joined them for short periods but these two carried on the work, taking turns in visiting the outlying missions while one remained at home to take care of Bayfield and vicinity. In 1881 they received the help of Fathers Eustace Vollmer and Odoric Derenthal, and, in 1883, Fathers Paulinus Tolksdorf and Chrysostom Verwyst arrived. On one of his visits to the Gordon mission, Father Odoric baptized Philip Bergin Gordon.

About the time of Philip's birth, the area also saw the completion of several railroads and the missionaries were able to travel more at ease and visit additional missions along the route.

By the time Philip was born, the country stood poised at the beginning of another era which would completely change the life of the Indians. Already the stage coach route had come and gone. It had followed the old St. Croix Trail that Father Gordon's ancestors knew so well. A series of narrow footpaths, blazed by the Indians many years ago through virgin forests, the Trail formed a land route over the two hundred miles from Lake Superior to Stillwater, Minn., a journey that required about ten days traveling.

Fallen trees and growth of jack pine and shrubs have filled the rutted, sandy wheel tracks, but faint traces of the old Trail could still be seen in 1975.

CHAPTER
II

Ancestry

~~~~~~

FAMOUS HISTORICAL CHARACTERS WERE AMONG REVEREND Philip Gordon's ancestors. In 1636, John Dingley migrated from England to Massachusetts. His daughter, Mary, married a son of Miles Standish. Seven generations later, Daniel Dingley married Isabella La Prairie (Musk-Ko-Dence) who was half French and half Chippewa Indian. Isabella was the daughter of a clerk for the Northwestern Fur Company mentioned in Curot's Journal for 1803-04.

Sarah, one of Daniel and Isabella's five children, became Philip's grandmother. Sarah was born in 1827 at Cadot's trading post at the mouth of the Yellow River in what is now Burnett County, Wis.

When Sarah was a young girl the family prepared for a long journey to a new home in St. Joseph, Mich., on the east shore of Lake Michigan. They were careful in the construction of a canoe for the journey. It must be light as possible because there would be many portages where Sarah's father would carry the canoe over paths through forests abounding in pine, spruce, fir, and birch. Isabella would pack a few belongings on her back.

Game, fish, and berries were plentiful, available for the taking, so there would be no need to carry many provisions. They would take some wild rice from the previous year's crop and a supply of furs for trade at posts along the way. Mink was plentiful and cheap but Dingley had other furs — muskrat, beaver, otter — but especially fox which was the most valuable at the time.

Dingley was fortunate in being in an area where birch was readily available. It was the most satisfactory material for a canoe, being light and pliable. A completed craft was easily carried by one man.

It was necessary to cut down the tree to obtain the thick sheets of bark for a canoe. When the family made their preparations, it was spring and the bark was at its best for canoe building.

Daniel was experienced in canoe construction. He had prepared material in advance. Several days before, he had split cedar trees and these were soaking so they would be ready for the framework when needed. He began making the canoe by laying out the birchbark sheets. He placed a wooden frame on them and held them down with stones. Then he bent up the edges and drove posts into the ground around the outside to hold the sides in place.

When he put in the cedar gunwales, Isabella made holes around the edge with an awl made of quartz and then sewed them in place with strings she had prepared from spruce roots. Ribs were fashioned from the cedar they had soaking. Daniel then inserted braces, known as thwarts, to rigidly hold the sides in place.

While they worked, spruce gum was being heated. They used this to seal the seams and make them watertight. They would take along a good supply of spruce gum to make repairs along the way. In an emergency, the gum could be chewed to soften it instead of being heated.

Now they had a craft like that of which Hiawatha said, "I, a light canoe will build me . . . that shall float upon the river, like a yellow leaf in autumn, like a yellow waterlily!"

The family traveled much of the summer to reach their new

home. The rivers, which were rushing torrents when they began their journey, gradually slowed to a calm rhythm as summer advanced.

When the Dingleys reached St. Joseph, Daniel opened a large trading post. In what Father Gordon later described in some handwritten notes as a "religious arrival (or revival)" — even after being highly educated, Father Gordon was noted for his poor penmanship — Daniel Dingley and his partner, "with a written form of self-dedication to God, brought the Indian women with whom they had been living according to Indian custom, and were legally married" in 1829.

One day Daniel Dingley packed a deerskin pouch with some wild rice, loaded his powder horn and shot pouch, shouldered his rifle and started out on a hunting expedition. He was never heard from again.

The family stayed at St. Joseph for a time, then moved to La Pointe on Madeline Island in Chequamegon Bay on Lake Superior.

Sarah had experienced the ceremonial fast and isolation as every young Indian girl did when she reached the age of sexual eligibility and adult importance according to her Indian mother's tradition. She had learned many skills from her mother. She learned to weave, tan hides, make articles of birchbark, and how to gather and prepare wild foods.

Sarah was a dark-eyed sixteen-year-old when she met the enterprising French and Indian fur trader, Antoine Gaudin. Sarah was well prepared for her marriage to Antoine.

Antoine's father, Jean Baptiste Gaudin, who was Philip's great-grandfather, was a Frenchman who was born at Trois Rivières in the Province of Quebec. He was employed as a voyageur from La Pointe. He roamed the forests as far west as Mille Lacs in what is now Minnesota. While there he married A-We-Ni-Shan (Young Beaver) a sister of Hole-In-The-Day, the Elder. This was the beginning of Philip Gordon's Indian heritage. A-We-Ni-Shan's nephew, Hole-In-The-Day, the Younger, (Pug-O-Ne-Gi-Jik), became a noted figure in Minnesota history. He was the acting head chief while Buffalo was hereditary chief of the Chippewa or Ojibway tribe.

When Antoine was twelve years old he went to Sault Sainte Marie, Mich. with his family. A few years later they returned to La Pointe where the American Fur Company had its headquarters under Michel Cadot, the "Great Michel" as the Indians called him. Michel fraternized with the Indians and married Equaysayway, the daughter of Chief White Crane; but like the other traders, he exploited the Indians, buying the raw furs at ridiculously low prices. Michel Cadot did business of about $40,000 annually.

Antoine married Sarah Dingley and in 1845 he opened a trading post and remained at La Pointe for ten years. Besides the post, he acquired an interest with Vincent Roy of Superior in the schooner, *Algonquin*. The ship had been built in 1839 at Black River, Ohio, now known as Lorain, for the Ohio Fishing & Mining Company. In 1845 it had been portaged around the Soo Rapids by the use of timbers and rollers, block and tackle, and ox teams.

Although there had been other sailing vessels on Lake Superior before the *Algonquin*, she was the first one of importance to carry cargo on the lake. Gaudin hauled logs from the Bad River area and returned with lumber and supplies for his trading post at La Pointe.

Antoine moved his family to a farm near the present site of Washburn in 1855 when William, who would become Philip's father, was only five years old. He eventually sold his interest in the *Algonquin* and in 1860, he led a group of French and Indians in two long, slim birchbark canoes down the St. Croix River.

The St. Croix and its tributaries had long been a trade route and war path of the Chippewa and Sioux tribes. The last great battle between the two rivals was fought on the St. Croix. The river ran red with Sioux blood when the Chippewa Chief Buffalo and his warriors, although fewer in number, outwitted and defeated the Sioux.

Gaudin proceeded to St. Croix near the mouth of the Snake River, taking a stock of goods for trade with the Indians. Cadot had a post there as well as at Yellow River and Pokegema Lake to the west. (You will remember the Yellow River post was the birthplace of Sarah, grandmother of Father Gordon.)

Although the population in the southern part of the state was growing at a rapid rate, northwestern Wisconsin was still an untamed wilderness, covered by seemingly inexhaustible pine forests. The pines thrived on the light, sandy soil deposited in the St. Croix Valley by the glaciers. There were less than six people per square mile.

Lumbermen looked longingly at the vast north woods but transportation of timber was impossible. The Indians had lived here for centuries, sustained by the resources of forest, lakes, and streams. They lived in harmony with Nature, or existed at its mercy, taking of its abundance only what they needed for their survival. If they exhausted the resources of one area they had but to move on to better hunting grounds and the area they left was soon replenished.

When the lumbermen penetrated the densely forested area they found that white pine was the most prized for lumber. It was easy to work with and was light and easily transported. Before the coming of the railroads all the logs were floated down the rivers. Pine would float, whereas the hardwoods sank to the bottom.

Historians referred to the area as the Folle Avoine Sauteur (literally, Wild Oats Jumping). The wild oats was actually wild rice, not a grain at all but a type of grass which grew profusely in the shallows along the rivers. The Indians said wild rice must grow with its feet in the water and its head dry.

Gaudin later planted rice for the Indians at Mulligan Lake, and he is known as the first conservationist. His descendants have harvested wild rice ever since; more than five thousand pounds a year have been taken from this lake. Some of his plantings can still be seen.

Antoine stayed for a while at Lost Post; but with the lumber business in mind, in 1862 he landed at the junction of the Eau Claire and St. Croix rivers at a place the Indians called Amick (the Beaver). He sold his interests at La Pointe and purchased forty acres of land from the Wisconsin Land and Improvement Company and the Henry Rice Land Company.

The log building Gaudin erected on the Eau Claire River was his home and trading store and became a boarding house for travelers as well. Winters were severe and often a time of want and privation with below-zero temperatures and deep snow. Gaudin gave shelter to Indians who were in need. He became their counselor and spokesman and acted as mediator between the wandering bands.

Some of the trade goods for the store were hauled from St. Paul by ox team or horses, bumping along the stage route over stumps and ruts. The stage line had been established in 1860 through the wilderness by widening the old foot trails.

The alternate route was up the Brule from La Pointe, navigating the canoes for about thirty-five miles, then carrying them over the Brule-St. Croix Portage, a distance of two miles over a pine ridge.

During their necessary long absences, the missionaries urged the people to build a chapel or church where they could meet. Anton Gordon, familiarly known as Tony, paid most of the expenses in the construction of a little log church in Gordon in 1874.

Recognizing the need of education for the children, he erected a log building in 1883, across from the trading post, next to the church. Here he taught both white and Indian children to read and write during the week and provided religious instruction on Sunday. Gordon had only three months of formal schooling, but he believed in education and had learned to speak English, French, and Chippewa. He also read Latin and understood the Sioux tongue.

Gordon's contact with the brown-robed Franciscans was largely responsible for his education. When he was a young man in La

Pointe he had been choir master and interpreter for Bishop Baraga, the famous missionary. The Bishop had written a grammar and dictionary of the Chippewa language.

It was only through the influence of his Indian mother that Anton did not pursue his aspiration to become a priest, a dream fulfilled many years later by his grandson, Philip.

Before his death in 1907, Tony Gordon had served three years as the first postmaster of Gordon; he was the town supervisor for six years and school treasurer for ten years. He was healthy and alert in his old age and operated the store until 1905.

Tony Gordon hired George Stuntz, who surveyed much of the territory, to lay out a town. When the Northwestern Railway was built in 1882, Gordon deeded the right-of-way and a depot was built. Around the turn of the century a village was established and named for its first settler, Tony Gordon. His wife, Sarah, was often called upon to act as midwife and on some occasions she was transported by hand car on the Northwestern Railway.

This was the place to which William Gordon had come as a child with his parents, and where he married his Indian wife and fourteen children were born to them. Among them were seven sons, of whom Philip was the youngest. This was the village where Philip began the life which was to take him far from his wilderness home. He became the friend of the great and famous in all walks of life — statesmen, cardinals, soldiers, scientists, businessmen, and people of all nations.

Philip's Indian name, "Ti-Bish-Ko-Gi-Jik," meaning "Looking into the Sky" was prophetic of his life's calling as a "Sky Pilot." Did he plan his career as a young boy? Catherine Gordon McDonald tells this story:

"My dad was Father Gordon's brother, Joe. They lived out in the country and they went into town one day. Phil was supposed to stay with the younger children. When his parents came home, some of the children were crying. Phil had taken the curtains off the windows and made himself a priest's robe. The children said, 'Ma, Phil made us pray all day.' "

CHAPTER
III

Indian Childhood

~~~~~~

WHEN PHILIP BERGIN GORDON WAS BORN IN 1885, HIS
grandfather was doing a thriving business at the trading post. During
his childhood Phil enjoyed visiting the store with its colorful
array of goods displayed for trade with the Indians.

Me-Sa-Bi would be there too. He made his home with his sister,
A-Te-Ge-Kwe, who was Philip's mother. Although Joe Mesabi was
Phil's uncle, their ages were close and they became pals.

William Gray Purcell describes the Gordon place in his book,
St. Croix Trail Country. One of his characters in the book, Gordon
Young says, "You know old Antoine built that place of his before
northern Wisconsin had even been surveyed and mapped. That
was about 1843." (The date is incorrect.) "When the Trail was
cut through he added a porch to his store and built the sleeping
rooms and kitchen and eating room across the road. Just north
of his hotel, he made a fine church with straight logs, square-faced
inside and out and tenoned at the corners like his store. This was
the way Father Baraga had taught him, to build all things with
respect. The wood, the tools, and the skills were those of age-old
Wendish carpenters, artist-axemen of the Baltic North.

19

"He set up an outdoor Shrine of Music in the churchyard —
four satin-smooth peeled poles, six yards in length, to be for a
belfry. These he canted like a sort of tripod to form a seat for the
swinging bell at the top of it. He also made a sheltering roof with
long, clean, split shakes. These he pegged, making good projection
for its eaves. He painted it all white and the church too, within
and without, and on the peak of his belfry was a cross which he
painted yellow.

"Amazing fellow, Old Man Gordon."

Orrin McGrath, who lived as a boy at Trego, twenty-four miles
south of Gordon, remembers the old store with its walls and ceiling
blackened by smoke from the fireplace and the early methods of
lighting. In the very early times, before the coming of the railroad,
various methods of lighting were used, depending on what was
most available. Torches were made of pine needles and pitch, or
pine knots, which could be found where a tree had fallen and
decayed. Candles were made of deer tallow placed in a dish with
a piece of wool yarn or cloth twisted and used for a wick. But
mostly, the traders depended on daylight.

After the railroad came through, kerosene lanterns hanging
from the ceiling provided somewhat better lighting. McGrath
remembers when Gordon got a stove and blocked up the fireplace
around 1903 or 1904.

Phil and Joe were accustomed to the air in the store, heavy
with the pungent, musky odor of hides hanging from pegs around
the room, mingling with the fragrant burning logs, tobacco, and
wet clothing drying by the fireplace.

When the post was built, lumber had to be hauled long distances
from the nearest mill, and so there were not many shelves in the
store. Many supplies, such as flour, beans, molasses, were hauled
in wooden barrels which were made by hand. These stood on
the floor. Maple sugar was left in the birchbark containers in
which the Indians had brought it. There was tea, and later coffee,
blankets, bolts of calico in bright colors, a few guns, traps, axes,
and brilliantly colored beads and trinkets which appealed to the

Indians. They wore mostly deerskin clothing, but as time went on such articles as shirts and pants were added to the stock.

The trading post was an exciting place for two little boys. They had continuous contact with older Indians at the store. The Indians revealed to Phil and Joe many tales and legends of their ancestors — battles with their traditional enemies, the Sioux; how the Chippewa had defeated them; they heard how Phil's father, when he was only twelve years old, went with his father to Minnesota to convince Pug-O-Ne-Gi-Jik, (Hole-In-The-Day) the war chief, not to go along with the Sioux against the white people.

Hole-In-The-Day was often bold and impudent and there were reports that the Chippewa chiefs had held a council with the Sioux, had settled their old differences, and were planning a simultaneous attack.

Antoine Gaudin went from the present Gordon, over a hundred miles, down the St. Croix River by canoe, and then by horseback into Minnesota and persuaded his cousin not to join the Sioux nation in the uprising that resulted in the bloody New Ulm and Mankato massacres. The towns were burned and several hundred settlers were killed. The affair ended with the greatest mass hanging in the history of the United States. After much deliberation, President Lincoln released many Indians, but he signed the death warrant for thirty-eight Sioux, who were hanged and buried at Wood Lake. But the lives of perhaps hundreds of white people were saved by Gaudin's action.

Philip's father, William, had gone as far as Rush City and rode back the one hundred miles through the wilderness, alone.

The boys heard tales of the voyageurs, Phil's brave, bronzed, French ancestors with their bright caps and scarves and flamboyant airs, who mingled with the Indians and did much to pave the way for civilization.

Mail and supplies were now transported by train, but the boys heard stories about how Phil's father, when a young man, had carried mail on the route from Gordon to Bayfield, the last leg of the Stillwater to Bayfield route. He traveled only during the summer as his father would not let the boy tackle the trip during the severe winter months with below zero temperatures and many feet of snow.

Often the mail went through only once a month during the winter when transportation was on snowshoes or with a dog team.

William would leave Gordon at three or four o'clock in the morning and travel on foot all day along the narrow trail through the dense woods. His little pure white dog, which always accompanied him, helped him many times to find the way as it walked ahead of him through the dark, early morning hours.

With the heavy pack on his back, William would reach his destination in the late afternoon or early evening. The route led past Ox Creek and on to the Halfway House at Spider Lake. He traveled about thirty-five miles in the undisturbed wilderness of dark pine woods to the half-way point between Gordon and Bayfield. The remainder of the way, the mail was carried by Mr. Busquet (or Buskey), whose uncle operated a trading post at Spider Lake. He also made the trips in winter when he could. There were times when he had to plod ahead of the dogs to break a trail.

South of Gordon, William's brother, Edward, who had a post on the Nemakagon River, carried the mail. From there it was relayed to Sunrise and Rush City, Minn., and then transported by rail to St. Paul.

If the mail from Bayfield was already at Spider Lake, William would make the return trip the next day. If there were delays, he would have to wait over at the Halfway House before returning to Gordon. Although the route through the forest was dangerous, Gordon was never armed and he never had an accident. He recalled that Mr. Buskey had a close call one evening when he encountered a pack of wolves. Buskey also had a small dog for company. He grabbed his dog and climbed a tree for safety. The mail pouch, which sometimes weighed seventy pounds, was too heavy so he dropped it to the ground at the foot of the tree where it was torn to bits by the savage wolves. Buskey remained in the tree with his dog until nearly daylight when the wolves left the scene.

Phil's father told the boys of trips he made with his father during the early days when travel was extremely difficult. Tony Gordon would go by ox team to St. Croix to buy furs, which was more important than money in trade. William recalled a time when a grain bag stuffed full of money was tossed on a wagon and handled the same as if it had been a bag of potatoes.

The two little Indian boys were being indoctrinated into the tribal customs and the mysteries of the Medicine Men. One day Me-Sa-Bi would take the place of Osawati, the chief shaman of the tribe because tribal heritage was carried on through the female line, and Me-Sa-Bi had been adopted by his sister.

But they were also being educated in the ways of the white man in the new one-room school that had replaced the original log structure built by Phil's grandfather. With a later addition, this school would stand until 1933 when it was destroyed by fire. The boys would live to see many schools built in Gordon and the surrounding district.

Tales of the lumberjacks, who were now coming to the store, were equally fascinating to the boys. The tide of immigration had set in. The prairie country to the west was being settled and the demand for lumber from the immense pine forests was strong. The logs were hauled by ox teams to the river banks and floated down the St. Croix River to St. Croix Falls and Stillwater, Minn., which became the terminals for timber cut all around the area.

As Phil heard more of the outside world, he began to realize, even at his early age, that the Indians were not living as well as others.

Mauser-Sauntry and Weyerhauser had large camps in the vicinity of Gordon, Wascott, and Solon Springs. Gordon became the chief supply point for these camps in the winter and for the drives in the spring. Lumberjacks going into the big woods to cut logs, took with them horses, oxen, beans, flour, hay, whiskey, canthooks, axes, saws, salt pork, and sourdough.

Early settlers in the East had learned through experience that they could not afford to use timber of inferior quality in their farm buildings, their churches, or the fortifications they built for protection from the Indians. When they moved west, the lumber industry had no choice but to cut the best logs and leave the inferior timber in the woods. Much was wasted and often burned. Although they have been condemned for their practices, there was demand only for quality lumber. It was the price we paid for the development of our nation.

A journey of a few miles with a team of oxen was a slow and tedious process through unbelievably dense growth. The pioneers could not foresee the end of the magnificent forests that extended beyond imagination.

Times were changing rapidly with the growing lumber business and the dwindling fur supply. In 1897, William Gordon moved his large family to the Court Oreilles Reservation in Sawyer County, which was the area where his Indian wife had lived. From there they went to Odanah on the Bad River Reservation and another phase in the life of Philip Gordon began.

CHAPTER IV

Life on the Reservation

~~~~~~

IT WAS JUNE, 1897, WHEN WILLIAM GORDON ARRIVED WITH his family at the Bad River Reservation. Tall, straight pines with their solid canopy of branches still shaded the soft, deep carpet of needles, the accumulation of centuries, but they were rapidly disappearing. The beaver too, which had been the standard by which the value of goods was rated, were also being depleted due to overtrapping, lack of their favorite food, the birch and aspen, and also from disease.

Philip Gordon and Joe Mesabi would be separated for the first time. They would miss each other but both were busy learning many skills from indulgent parents, sisters, brothers, and respected older members of the tribe.

The boys were encouraged to fast while still young and to reveal their dreams so that they would know what to look for when the time came for their trial when they would find a spirit to guide them through life.

Mesabi had taken his vision quest and Philip had been conditioned by an occasional fast so when, late that summer, he went into the forest, he was ready for his manhood trial. Fasting had supposedly cleared his mind and Philip pondered the possibility of Mesabi one day becoming a chief of the tribe. Although his mind was receptive, his visions were confused.

He dreamed of many things out there in the lonely forest, but his dreams had no significance. Mesabi knew he was designated to follow Osawati; but when Phil returned home after four days, his quest was unresolved. He had found no spirit to guide him through life. The Christian faith of his grandfather was in conflict with the old Indian traditions.

The hot summer was passing quickly with many things to do and now it was August. Soon the harvest moon would be shining over the Bad River and ricing time would be here. Rice was one of the most important items of food among the Chippewas, and so a good harvest was important to them.

When the top of the grass began to turn yellow, the Indian women would go out to bind the stalks into sheaves. A-Te-Ge-Kwe had prepared basswood fiber from the inner bark of the tree to be used for tying. She had split the long strips, tied them together and rolled them into a ball. When she went into the rice fields in her canoe, she wore a special waist with a birchbark basket behind her back to hold the ball of twine. The fiber was passed through little birchbark rings on her shoulder so it was always ready and would not become tangled.

With a "rice hoop," a branch curved and secured with strips of fiber, A-Te-Ge-Kwe would draw a cluster of rice stalks toward her and wind the fiber around them, bending the tip of the bundle down. This would protect the rice from birds, wind, and floods until the tops turned purple. Then it would be time for harvesting.

Phil eagerly anticipated the rice harvest. It was a time of festivities. Entire family groups established camps for several weeks and all helped during the process.

In the meantime, there were geese and ducks to be shot or snared before they migrated to the south. A-Te-Ge-Kwe and the other women prepared green deerhide, placing it over a log and scraping the hair from it.

A-Te-Ge-Kwe was a small woman. When Philip was grown, she only reached to his shoulder. He was a full head taller. But she had the strength and agility of her ancestors and worked right along with the other women.

Phil liked to watch the women as they cut the hide into strips, wove them into nets and placed them in the rice fields. They sometimes caught forty geese at one time. These they prepared and smoked for winter use.

When the rice was ready, usually a man and a woman went out in a canoe. The man had the strenuous job of slowly poling the canoe through the water with a forked pole, skillfully guiding it between the rows of tied bundles. The woman sat in the stern of the canoe and rhythmically beat the stalks on each side to knock off the rice kernels.

When the canoe was filled, they brought it to the camp. First, they picked out by hand the pieces of dry stalks and debris that had fallen in with the rice. Then they spread the rice on large blankets to dry, being careful not to put it directly in the sun where it could overheat.

These were good times for Phil and his friends. In later years he returned at every opportunity for the ricing.

The next step, parching, was a critical one. One of the women put a few pounds of rice at a time in a big kettle over the fire. She had propped her kettle in a slightly slanting position so she could sit on a rush mat and stir the rice with a slender paddle. The fire had to be well regulated and the rice constantly stirred so it would not burn.

Many family camps were processing rice at the same time. Phil would always remember the rich, zesty aroma that hung over the area when the parching fires blended with the maple-sugar flavored meat stewing for the evening meal.

Parching loosened the husks, cured the rice, and gave a nutlike flavor. It was a slow and tedious process but it was the best method. Another method was producing what was known as "hard rice," which was greenish black, much darker than parched rice and required longer to cook. This method was similar to drying berries. A layer of hay was placed on a rack and the rice spread on it and dried over a slow fire.

During the parching, the women had winnowing trays beside the fire into which they emptied the parched rice. Others would take it to a spot where there was a breeze to blow the chaff when they poured the rice onto a sheet of birchbark on the ground.

The next step, known as "pounding" the rice, was not really pounding, which would destroy the kernels. In a barrel or wooden container of rice, a wooden pestle about five and a half feet long was dropped carefully around the outer edge of the container to free the husk from the kernel.

This year, Phil would help with "dancing the rice." He put on the moccasins that had been made for the purpose and tied them tightly around his ankles while A-Te-Ge-Kwe placed some rice in the barrel which was sunk into the ground. Leaning on the diagonal poles on each side, Phil performed a sort of dance which would dislodge the last fragments of husks without harming the kernels. The chaff was also saved and cooked like the rice. The Indians took pride in carefully carrying out each step of the ricing process.

There would be rice, seasoned with maple sugar, for the evening meal, along with the fish the women had caught in their net that morning and the rabbit the boys had hunted, already stewing over the campfire.

After a long day of hard work, there was dancing and drumming on the shore at night when all the families, who had not seen each other for months, got together. These events would forever be burned into Phil's memory and were an influence later in his life.

Many preparations were made for the long, severe winter months. All during the summer the Indian families had been gathering berries, fruits, and herbs to preserve and dry for the winter. Later they would travel to the cranberry bogs to harvest the berries to dry. These, or sometimes blueberries, were used to make pemmican. They were mixed with chopped venison and smoked, the stomach of a deer being used as a casing. This would keep a long time and was handy to take along on a trip.

Most of the garden vegetables — corn, squash, potatoes — were already stored away. The Indians lacked many luxuries but there were festivities to enjoy and good food when the harvest was plentiful.

CHAPTER
V

Murder and "Buried Gold"

THERE WAS OTHER EXCITEMENT DURING THE SUMMER. WILLIAM Gordon had come to Odanah, not as a great Indian chief, but as Chief of the Indian Police and interpreter at the Indian Agency. During his first year as chief, he had the unpleasant duty of arresting his own uncle.

Joseph Blackburn and his brother, John, had come from Cincinnati, Ohio, to Stillwater, Minn., in 1847. They went into business together and traded all over Minnesota and into Wisconsin. Later they split up. John went to work for the Shell Lake Lumber Company and Joe opened a trading post about ten miles southeast of Gordon in 1860. He married Mary Dingley, sister of Sarah, Philip's grandmother.

Joe was accused of trespass in his transactions for timber rights when he allegedly hauled lumber off government lands. A warrant was given to Bill Gordon which he served on his uncle. He took Joe to Madison and testified against him in Federal Court. Blackburn was fined $10,000. He wrote a check for that amount on the First National Bank of Stillwater. The court, being skeptical, wired the bank. The answer came back, "Blackburn's check up to $50,000 will be honored."

Blackburn came to a tragic end, no doubt due to his wealth. On October 1, 1897, he returned from the Eau Claire Lakes with a wagon load of cranberries. He had unhitched his horses from the wagon but had not yet removed the harnesses, when he was apparently attacked by an unknown assailant. Evidence showed indications of a fight and Blackburn was killed by a blow on the head with a blunt instrument. His axe, which had been fastened to his wagon with leather thongs, was found near his body and was either the murder weapon or he had used it in defending himself. The crime has never been solved.

The story was revived in 1932 when the Superior *Evening Telegram* published an article, "Pioneer Sheds Light on 'Buried Gold' Narrative." The paper had received a letter from Frank Berquist, pioneer Gordon resident and an old friend of Blackburn.

The letter stated, "A man who gave his name as Akerly and his residence as Minnesota, recently told District Attorney Claude Copper that he had been told by 'spirits' that there was gold in an Indian squaw's grave at Gordon, Wis.

"Akerly's story was connected with Blackburn's death by courthouse employees, for although Blackburn was reputed to be a wealthy man, after his death none of his wealth was ever found. . . . From time to time since Blackburn's death, stories have been circulated as to the whereabouts of the money Blackburn was supposed to have and now some persons believe the money is in his wife's coffin."

Father Gordon, who was at Centuria, Wis., at the time the above item was published, wrote, "Joe Blackburn was quite a figure in his time. When his wife Mary died, seven years before his death occurred, Blackburn erected a chapel into which eight or ten persons could pass with seats arranged so that visitors could sit while viewing the closed coffin. Her grave was never filled up and I often wondered how evidence of corruption did not make it impossible to enter the chapel."

It was an old Indian custom to build a little wooden house about five feet long and two or three feet high over a grave with a place for food offerings. Some of these may still be seen in northern Wisconsin and Minnesota. Blackburn's was much larger than that.

After reading the newspaper article, Father Gordon wrote, "My father often related incidents pertaining to Blackburn's wealth. On one occasion, after a winter's logging, Blackburn came home to Gordon bearing a small oaken chest under his arm. My father saw therein hundreds of bills, greenbacks of various denominations, and estimated there was easily several thousand dollars in the box.

"It is my father's opinion that the money of Joe Blackburn, who lived almost a miser's existence, dressing poorly, traveling very little and never known to have any immediate relatives other than a brother, is somewhere on the premises formerly occupied by Blackburn. The idea that Blackburn hid his treasure, if he had any, in the coffin of his deceased wife sounds improbable but would not have been impossible."

Mr. Berquist, in his letter, added, "Blackburn was one of the most picturesque and best liked of the early settlers in the vicinity of Gordon. . . .

"Blackburn did not live in a shack, but in a large hewed timber building, which had accommodations for forty men or more and this building still stands" (1932). "Lumberjacks going to and from the camps, used to stop at the Blackburn place and there were several other good sized buildings on the land, one being used as a trading post. . . . Blackburn was a man who did not have much to say but always helped anyone in need."

CHAPTER
VI

Happy Reunion

~~~~~~

THE EXCITEMENT OF SUMMER ENDED ALL TOO SOON. THE school term began in September and Philip was attending St. Mary's Mission School at Odanah. The Franciscans had obtained government permission to build a school in 1881. The Indians, including Protestants and pagans, felled trees and hewed logs to erect a little log school which opened in 1883 with two Franciscan Sisters from La Crosse, Wis., as teachers. During the next two decades, no less than eight additions were built.

By the time Philip Gordon entered the school, Father Chrysostom had obtained some government help and the school became a boarding school as well as a day school.

Phil received First Communion and Confirmation and was in contact with Franciscan Fathers. His health was not good at this time and some of his family had already died of tuberculosis, which was prevalent in the Indian communities.

Gradually the scenery changed to amber and tan with splashes of brilliant red, purple, and gold. White birch with their shimmering golden leaves stood out against the dark green pines.

A touch of autumn was in the air and again it would be ricing time; but the long, severe winter lay ahead.

Phil was a good student and liked to study; but he looked forward to spring, for in March the Indian families would travel to the sugar bush. This would be another time of festivity, and it would also be a reunion with Joe Mesabi.

Indians had been gathering the sweet maple sap for centuries. Historians believe they only partly reduced the sap to the form of a sweet liquid which was used as a medicine.

The *Jesuit Relations* tell how an early missionary, hearing that a pagan Indian was near death, visited his wigwam and administered the last rites of the Church.

After baptizing him from a bark vessel in the room, he inquired of the man's wife what medicine the patient had been taking. The woman pointed to the vessel. The priest discovered he had performed the baptism with sweet maple syrup. Fortunately, the patient lived until the priest secured water and performed the ceremony again.

When the sugaring season arrived, the women went ahead to prepare the camp. They traveled on snowshoes and carried rolled sheets of birchbark by a pack strap across their foreheads. The pack was not heavy but it made a rather awkward, towering package. It must have been overwhelming on one as small as A-Te-Ge-Kwe.

The lodge framework had been left from the previous year and the women laid sheets of bark on the roof, fastening them with deerskin thongs. Inside, on a platform they spread cedar boughs on which they laid rush mats, blankets, and furs. Here is where the family would sleep during their stay in the sugar bush.

Next, they turned back the rolls of birchbark on the storehouse and inspected the utensils that had been stored there since the last season, to see what would be needed. They were now using metal pails and iron kettles for cooking the sap in place of the birchbark utensils of their ancestors. The Indians had taught the French how to collect and reduce the sap and the French in turn introduced the iron kettle and so improved the process.

The metal utensils had been taken home after the previous season and would be brought to the camp later. But they still used some of the birchbark makuks. These were always scrubbed with wood ashes and a stone at the end of the season, then stacked together, tied, and stored upside down in the storehouse. Some of these makuks had to be mended with balsam or spruce gum so they would not leak.

There were many chores to be done in preparation for collecting sap and when these were completed the women returned home for their families.

What a happy reunion for Phil and Joe! They had so many things to talk about but they were growing up and were able to help with the work of gathering sap. Sunny days and frosty nights had started the sap running, but there was still snow on the ground. On snowshoes, the boys went happily from tree to tree to help insert the wooden spouts which had been whittled from sumac branches in the late winter. They suspended a bucket beneath each spout to collect the sap.

Each day they plodded through the woods to collect the sap and bring it to the kettle hanging over the fire. But the Indians took their work and recreation together and there was feasting and dancing along with the work.

Since Phil had last seen him, Mesabi had learned many of the arts from Osawati. Most of the Indians were taking French or English names, which they sometimes mispronounced so that they had a distinctive sound. Surnames were often acquired because they were needed on the payroll records of the lumber camps where they worked. Some of the names were translated from their Indian names, like Hole-In-The-Day and Little Buffalo.

Osawati had taken his name when he took his trial to become a warrior and had never Americanized it because he was the chief medicine man or shaman of the tribe. Mesabi, too, preferred to be called by his Indian name as he was being trained to replace Osawati.

Like most Indians, they believed in a Supreme Being, a mystic supernatural force which permeated all Nature and was called Manitou. They looked on the earth and its trees, fruits, and animals as gifts from the Great Spirit, and believed in spiritual beings who were the personification of elements in Nature.

Mesabi was learning to call upon these spirits when healing herbs or other curative agents were administered. The cure was accomplished with ceremony, incantations, songs, and prayers to the spirits.

Osawati, as shaman, was above the other medicine chiefs and would always sit at the right of them at the councils. Mesabi would inherit this title and carry on the legendry to the next generation.

Philip had grown to be a handsome young man, slender and not very tall. His straight black hair was usually neatly combed. His black eyes were quite closely set in a very dark-skinned, broad face. His straight nose and slightly full lips and high forehead gave him an attractive, intelligent appearance.

When he was fifteen, Philip passed the county examination and received a teacher's certificate. The nuns at the school saw his potential and raised money so he could attend Superior State Normal for one year.

The paths of the two Indian boys were taking them farther and farther apart.

CHAPTER
VII

Indian Problems

WHILE PHILIP GORDON WAS GROWING UP THE SPIRIT LAND of the Ojibway was fast disappearing. The young man was soon to experience the discrimination and degradation suffered by his people, and with realization came a determination to help them.

When the railroad came, the Indian's way of life was doomed. The appalling factor was the swiftness and cruelty of it all. The sudden bewildering adjustment is hard for the white man to comprehend. In one generation the heavy forests which had supplied the Indian's home, his food, and his clothing, were swept away. In 1899 there were 1,033 sawmills in operation in Wisconsin and lumbermen cut 3,389,166,000 feet of lumber, more than two-thirds of which was white pine from the northern forests.

Philip Gordon was ambitious and worked to acquire the education he desired. He experienced life in a lumber camp during one winter where he helped with scaling and tallying. Later he worked for a period in a sawmill as a handyman, then tending a conveyor and picking slabs.

According to brief notes he jotted down late in his life, he was "fired and called down by George Moore, worked in company store for maybe two years. Delivery man and clerk. Sickness: Sore knee, poor health. Other manual labor: Timekeeper when government furnished funds for road repair."

The rough and rugged life in the woods apparently helped to improve his health. He became well known in the Chequamegon Bay District as a baseball player. His notes also include brief reminiscences of baseball players and teams — "The Silver Dollar Baseball Team. Bert Walker, Basil Gordon. The Red Shots. The North Stars. Jocko Starr, Swan, Ed. Walker, Hafaday, A. Gordon and Sharlow. To north of Bad River several times. While in Odanah went to Minneapolis to see the Wis. & Minn. game in the old Northrup Field with Dan Morrison and Mike Auge. The Pauly Hotel."

His baseball team competed with Arbor Vitae, Iron River, Washburn, Ashland, Saxon, Hurley, and Hayward. The last game he played before entering St. Thomas College was at Hayward against his cousin Carley.

These notes were little reminiscences that came to mind many years later and were rather rambling: "Two falls at public school. Teachers, Miss Dahrke or Mrs. Donohue. Away on Milwaukee trip for Donahue. Learned several Protestant hymns. Blessed Assurance. Annual Methodist Camp meeting. Rev. T. C. Thomas, Reverence for Men of God. Indian Medicine dances, Lost Lake. In Superior for Normal School during Odanah stay. At parties. To Gordon for first return visit."

Years later, Fred Holmes and Dan Wallace considered writing a book about the Indian priest and encouraged him to prepare an outline for a biography. They wrote, "Although he experienced the life of an adolescent in a lively Reservation Mill town, Philip never learned to dance, did not smoke and never tasted intoxicating liquor, looked upon as a 'good boy.' "

After a year at Superior, Phil attended Northland College at Ashland for a year. He established a friendship with his roommate and fellow athlete, Dan Brownell, who later became president of Northland College.

It was at the college that Phil became aware of girls. First there was Lena for a short time. Then Emma Heany. According to his notes, he dated Emma for two winters and one summer in Ashland. They enjoyed ice cream socials in the Old Council Hall, went to the circus, and picked berries on the Ashland Road.

One of his college friends, John Medegan, a theological student and also a Chippewa Indian, suggested St. Thomas College, St. Paul, Minn., to Philip.

There were other Indians, including some of Philip's brothers, who were recognizing the need of adopting the white man's life and receiving an education in various professions. One of his brothers would become a doctor, one a lawyer, and one a dentist.

Philip was concerned about the many Indians who could not be convinced they would have to change their way of life. Years later he was to say, "The Indian traditions must be preserved, but in books."

The early French traders had always been friendly with the Indians and found them to be honorable and faithful in keeping their treaties and other obligations. They realized their fur trading business depended on preserving the forests and their good relations with the Indians.

Later settlers, however, desired land and lumber. Years of controversy and broken treaties followed. They expected the Indian to change in a few years to a point of civilization which had taken their own ancestors centuries to accomplish.

By 1871 almost all of the Indian lands had been acquired. Most of the Indians were settled on reservations and repression was causing many problems — apathy, irresponsibility, drinking, and delinquency. The Allotment Act of 1887 was to be the final solution of the problem. Each family group would receive 180 acres of land which would be inalienable and tax free for a generation. By that time the Indians were expected to have broken tribal ties and turned into ordinary farmers like their white neighbors.

The government soon realized that some might need more than one generation to get started as farmers, and provisions were made requiring that the Indian be declared competent to farm before he acquired his land patent no matter how long the time since he got his allotment.

By 1900 Indian population had increased so that the allotments were divided among more and more heirs with people inheriting small pieces of different allotments, widely separated from another. They could not compete with the larger, mechanized farms which were increasing at this time. Once again the Indians were at the mercy of unscrupulous land grabbers.

In 1852, Luke Lea, Commissioner of Indian Affairs, had written:

"The embarrassments to which they (the Indians who resisted deportation and absorption) are subjected, in consequence of the onward pressure of the whites, are gradually teaching them the important lesson that they must ere long change their mode of life, or cease to exist at all. It is by industry or extinction that the problem of their destiny must be solved."

Now it seemed extinction would be the solution. Lea did not foresee the results of the crushed spirits of the Indians.

CHAPTER
VIII

College Days

PHILIP GORDON BELIEVED HE COULD HELP THE INDIANS AND
he was anxious to get on with his education. Although he loved
the old Indian traditions, he knew their way of life could not
survive in the modern world. If he could help them through his
ministry, he was ready to devote his life to it.

In the spring of 1903, he wrote a letter to the Provincial
Seminary of St. Francis, St. Francis, Wis. On March 22, he
received the following reply:

My Dear Philip Gordon,
I sent you our catalogue lately which contains all necessary
information concerning our institution. I also made inquiries
about you and am glad to say that you have been well recom-
mended although *doubts have been expressed concerning your
vocation to the holy priesthood.* (Underscoring by Father
Gordon.)
You did not mention anything concerning this point, so I
suppose you only wish to obtain a good secular or business
education. Still, if you have the intention and a strong desire
for the priesthood, you might try and come here, but as we

have no funds you would have to pay the whole amount of our tuition at least the first year. If you then give good satisfaction you might obtain some help from the "St. Francis League for indigent students."

In the meantime, I remain
Yours sincerely,
J. Rainer

Philip had been disturbed about the conditions facing the Indians, but now he felt his first awareness of racial discrimination against him personally as he read into the letter bias against him. He was really to learn about segregation later when he traveled in the South. His dark skin caused him to be relegated to the negro section. At one time he tried to secure a hotel room and there was none available. When it was learned he was an American Indian and not a negro the hotel suddenly found a room, but Father Gordon said, "No thanks."

At any rate, Phil did not have enough money to pay the tuition at St. Francis Seminary, so he worked to earn enough to enter St. Thomas Military College in St. Paul.

His college days were some of the happiest and most exciting of his life. He was popular and perfectly adjusted, with a reputation of being "rather a good student, exemplary in conduct."

He was not only a good student but he excelled in sports. He earned more letters in athletics than any student. He played football all through his college years. The roster of the squad in his first year could have been that of the "Fighting Irish." The list contained: Harrington, O'Hara, Cullen, Sherran, O'Shaughnessy, McGonigal, McHale, McDermott, Fitzgerald, Duggan, Kafferty, Carlin, Luedtke, Maloney, Dooley, Hoppenyan, Peschges, Cavannaugh, Dowd, Lang, Culleton, Coleman, Healy, Dougherty — and Gordon. Some of these became priests and at least one, a bishop. The team was quite impressive in their wide-striped, long-sleeved, turtle-necked jerseys, knee pants, and heavy knee socks.

Phil's name appeared often in the *St. Thomas Collegian*. The

April, 1905, edition stated, "Basketball was first introduced at St. Thomas in 1904. Philip Gordon was a member of that team. Whether at guard or forward, he played a brilliant game with that unassuming manner of his which so quickly wins the spectators. Many a time when our basket was in danger, Gordon reversed the situation like a flash, by driving the ball with his 'terrible left' straight and sure to O'Keefe at the other end of the gym."

In November, 1905, "Gordon played left end on the football team. He played strong defensive games."

In February, 1906, "Gordon received the letter 'S.T.' as a qualified member of the football team. He was manager of the baseball team. Played left end on the football team — a fast and heady game against the N. Dak. Aggies. In basketball, Gordon, left guard, was captain of the team."

In May of that year, "The basketball team won the pennant in the City League. It was captained by Gordon who played an excellent game throughout the winter and made an ideal leader. He was very aggressive and worked hard during any game until the whistle sounded."

And in December, "Gordon was the choice of many critics for an end position on the All Star Inter-Collegiate team."

His athletic career continued in 1907, along with other activities. In May the *Collegian* noted, "Gordon was one of five veterans in basketball. He was on the Committee of the Temperance Society. In the Military Department he was captain of Company C."

During this year he was saddened by the death of his grandfather, Anton Gordon, at the age of 95[1] who was buried in the cemetery overlooking the river on which he had established his trading post.

Philip's gift of oratory was showing up now in college. In

[1]There are discrepancies between records at Bayfield and Gordon. Dates on his tombstone are Jan. 10, 1812 - May 3, 1907.

February, 1908, the *Collegian* states, "The annual Thanksgiving entertainment was given under the auspices of the Senior Literary Society. Gordon gave an oration on Thanksgiving. As a left guard in basketball, Phil is energetic and always alert. His excellent guarding prevented opponents from shooting baskets."

In his graduation year, 1908, he was being recognized for his eloquence, probably inherited from the tribal orators in his ancestry. The *Collegian* reported: "In June, he was in the play, 'The Toastmaster.' The character of Towel Fairfax was interpreted in a masterful fashion by Philip Gordon. His smoothly eloquent speech and intellectual ways took well with the audience, by whom he was frequently applauded.

"In the Elocution Class final contest, Gordon gave Lew Wallace's 'The Chariot Race.'

"He was graduated from the Collegiate Dept. in 1908, receiving gold medal for general excellence. He received the Latin Special Merit award, first distinction in Greek and in English."

Phil spent his summer vacations at his parent's farm near Clear Lake in Sherburne County, Minn., where they had moved shortly after he entered St. Thomas. He played bush league baseball there. One of his teammates was Harold Knutson, who later became Congressman.

The vigorous program of sports at the college helped to give Philip the constitution necessary to withstand the dread tuberculosis which had already claimed three of his brothers and a sister.

During his years at St. Thomas his determination to become a priest was strengthened. He loved to study and he got his foundation there in the classics. He devoted much time to reading American history (which he says was written by white men).

During this time he spent one fall at Holy Cross College, Worcester, Mass., and found time to visit the St. Louis World Fair on the closing days. There he saw his first United States president, Theodore Roosevelt. He was to meet several more during his lifetime.

After graduating from St. Thomas College, Philip attended St. Paul Seminary, St. Paul, Minn., for one year. It was a delightful, fruitful year in the study of philosophy. Here he associated with 180 future priests.

CHAPTER
IX
Indian Allotments

~~~~~~

WILLIAM GORDON, THROUGH HIS WORK AS POLICEMAN, WAS thoroughly familiar with every spot on the reservation. Consequently, when the time came for Philip to receive his allotment, his father selected the most beautifully timbered stand of pine that remained. Many other Indians were not so fortunate, and Philip later helped in the fight to reclaim some of their losses.

Legally, the income from the timber cut on the land was his, but he was not allowed to spend it without the consent of the government agent on the reservation.

There was much confusion in regard to allotments and the use of the money. Contracts between the lumber companies and the Indian agencies were supposedly to insure that the funds derived from the sale of timber would come into the hands of the official representative of the government rather than into the possession of the chiefs who might be neglectful as to the distribution of the money among the members of the tribe or fail to use it for the benefit of the tribe.

Terms of the contracts were so loose and indefinite as to the amount of timber sold that it was impossible to protect the interest of the Indians adequately.

The treaty of 1854 had provided for the establishment of a residence upon the land by each person to whom an assignment was given in the hope that they would become self-supporting. But many problems and disputes arose, especially with the realization of the value of the pine timber on Indian reservations.

After inquiries from the Mississippi River Logging Company and Angus Cameron, an attorney at La Crosse, Wis., Secretary Henry M. Teller, on September 20, 1882, wired Cameron as follows: "If the Indians have patents they may sell the timber, subject to the approval of the Department, and the Department will approve contracts honorably and justly made."

On September 25, 1882, Mr. Cameron wrote: "The Indians are suspicious, and it is believed that few of them will sell or sign any contract of sale unless they are paid the whole consideration at the time of signing the contract."

Charges and investigations continued for years. On April 16, 1886, Special Agent H. Heth submitted a voluminous report, stating among other things, ". . . these Indians are well-clad and some of them have purchased good teams and have small farms. . . . The cash balances paid the Indians individually by the contractor, have been used, in some instances greatly to their benefit, but in many instances, as you would find among whites, has been squandered in the most useless geegaws, worthless trinkets, whiskey, and gambling with cards, which appears to be a favorite pastime with lazy and worthless Indians."

It was not difficult for unscrupulous loggers to make arrangements with some of these Indians for the sale of timber without government supervision, as they felt it was their right to dispose of the timber on reservation lands for their own benefit and many rebelled at the claims of the government to supervise all sales.

On July 1, 1898, Samuel W. Campbell, a veteran of the Civil War, became the Indian agent at Ashland in charge of the La Pointe Indian Agency. Two months later he wrote the Indian Office in Washington suggesting changes in payment of allotments, givng cash payments of $10.00 to $15.00 per month instead of $25.00 and $30.00 they had been paying.

Campbell wrote: ". . . I find many able-bodied Indians idle; neither working in the mills nor improving their allotments; but sitting idly down, folding their hands, eating and drinking up their allotments; and when it is all gone they will be much worse off than if they never had an allotment.

"Some of them have already spent every cent of their allotment and scores of others have their money almost gone, and in most of the cases they have nothing to show for their money. Thousands of dollars worth of orders have been issued against allotments not yet out, for teams and many other useless things which they did not need, and many of the teams have been starved, many disposed of for whatever they could get for them after the novelty had worn off. . . .

"In view of the above facts, and to better enable me to aid in saving the remnant of different allotments of the three reservations, I would recommend that you instruct me to not pay out any money on allotments to any able-bodied Indian who is able to work and earn his living, except for permanent improvements on their allotments; and to encourage them to improve their allotments, I would advise that for every acre they improve and clean up and cultivate, we pay them $10.00 or $15.00 of their money, and if they wish to make any other improvements, such as building, etc., to have it done through the Farmer and have him make estimates, thoroughly familiarizing himself with each application so he can give full information in detail, and see that everything goes for what the application calls. . . ."

Campbell went on in length, making allowances for the aged, widows, and minors, but cutting off indiscriminate payments to those able to work.

After five months deliberation, during which time Campbell had again written urging approval of his plan, the Indian Office notified him the plan would be given a trial, but was noncommittal and placed upon the agent most of the responsibility.

Agent Campbell became confused by later contradictory statements and inconsistencies in instructions which continued for years. As usual, investigations and controversies followed; finally, supervision of cutting was placed under the Bureau of Forestry. Later, criticism of this bureau by Assistant Government Farmer Norbert Sero in 1908 claimed that "representatives of the Bureau of Forestry, who marked the trees, selected the very largest and choicest white pine, contrary to the rules and regulations."

As Superintendent of Indian Affairs, Major Campbell became embroiled in almost continuous controversy and was accused of being obsessed with the idea that the Indians would almost invariably spend unwisely every dollar that came into their possession. Eventually, in 1912, he was dismissed when his administration was bitterly attacked by certain Indians through a Washington attorney. Many felt that great injustice was done him.

In view of all this contention, it is no wonder Philip Gordon felt a sense of futility when he approached Major Campbell. He realized Campbell, white and non-Catholic, undoubtedly would not grant his request to use the money he received for sale of timber to continue his studies for the priesthood.

In spite of accusations against him, Campbell's concern was the welfare of the Indians. Philip need not have worried for the agent readily gave his consent. He well knew the great need among the Indians for moral and spiritual help from someone who knew them.

Campbell was even helpful in cutting and marketing the timber on Philip's land and obtained $10,000 for the timber. The two became friends and later, when Major Campbell retired to his old home at Hudson, Wisconsin, Father Gordon frequently visited him.

Philip was at St. Paul Seminary in September, 1908, when forest fires burned over large areas on the Bad River Reservation. The fires temporarily slowed by rains but with drought conditions and accompanying high winds in the middle of October, the fires burned out of control again.

The amount of timber within the reservation injured by fire was estimated at from 50,000,000 to 100,000,000 board feet. More than 15,000,000 of this was on unallotted lands where no contract existed and the timber could be cut only under authority of the government. This was another subject of controversy for which Father Gordon later fought vigorously.

CHAPTER
X
Ordination and More Problems

~~~~~~

AFTER HE RECEIVED HIS ALLOTMENT, PHILIP GORDON WENT directly to the American College in Rome where he spent one year. He then attended the University of Innsbruck in Austria for two years.

The university was a typical German university, staffed by eminent professors. There was a large student body and many of Philip Gordon's schoolmates became bishops in Germany, Hungary, Austria, and several in the United States.

Philip enjoyed traveling and spent two summer vacation periods in France, Germany, Hungary, Austria, Switzerland, Holland, Belgium, and made one trip to England. Some of these were walking tours. In the land of his French ancestors, he learned to speak the language fluently and spent much of his time in the French department of Loir-et-Cher. Besides English and French, he spoke fluent German, Italian, and numerous Indian dialects.

Philip's vigorous schedule may have brought on a recurrence of his old ailment. He was forced to spend many weeks in a sanatorium in southern Tyrol as a suspected T. B. patient. He carried a scar the rest of his life from surgery on his neck at this time. His Roman collar covered the scar, and so few people were aware of it.

On his trips to France, he visited the shrine of the Little Flower, St. Therese of the Infant Jesus. It is to her he attributed the restoration of his health and numerous great favors. He said, "I have heard the living voices of the blood sisters of St. Therese." After his ordination he said Masses at her tomb.

Following his two years at Innsbruck, Phil returned to the United States and again attended St. Paul Seminary, where he studied Indian history and lore. He then spent several months at St. John's University at Collegeville, Minn., awaiting his ordination.

On December 8, 1913, the day for which he had been preparing all these years, finally arrived and he hoped he could now begin to help the downtrodden Indians. He was ordained in the cathedral in Superior, Wis., by the second bishop of the diocese, the Most Rev. Joseph Mary Koudelka, D.D.

When Father Gordon read his first Mass on January 6, 1914, at Odanah, on the Bad River Reservation, Father Odoric, the Franciscan missionary who had baptized Philip, preached the sermon at the Mass.

Father Gordon remained as an assistant Indian missionary for a short time in the diocese of Superior. Then, after serving a few months as pastor of a white parish at Hayward, Wis., he spent the next year at the Catholic University of America, Washington, D. C. Here he made lifelong friends of eminent professors, Dr. Kerby, Dr. Guilday, Dr. John A. Ryan, a former schoolmate at St. Paul Seminary, and others.

He encountered some problems as shown in the following letter he wrote on October 12, 1914, from the Apostolic Mission House at the University, to the vicar general of the Superior diocese, Very Rev. C. F. Schmit, asking for an extension of his leave of absence:

Very Rev. dear Father:

I write to inquire if you could, in some way or other, make arrangements with His Lordship for an extension of my leave of absence until I am able to finish my course at this University, or rather, at the Mission House. One of the original complaints of Father Odoric was that I did not prepare my sermons and His Lordship also mentioned the same disorder. I am here taking a special course in mission-work, sermon-writing in particular, as well as hours at the question-box in preparation for missions to non-Catholics.

I wish you would kindly communicate with me as soon as you have any definite information on the point I ask about. I will need to know a considerable time beforehand so that I can govern myself accordingly.

With kindest best wishes, believe me,

Yours very sincerely,
Philip B. Gordon

No matter where Father Gordon went, he made friends easily. While at the Catholic Uiversity, he also worked as a part time chaplain at Carlisle Institute in Pennsylvania. The school was founded in 1879 by Captain (later General) Pratt, who obtained from the army the use of Carlisle Barracks.

At the Institute Father Gordon became acquainted with Dr. Charles Eastman (Chiyesa), a Santee Indian who began his education without knowing one word of English. With the encouragement of his father, he walked 150 miles through the wilderness to enter the Santee Mission School in Nebraska, when he was about sixteen years old.

At a time when there was considerable hostility toward the Sioux nation, which included the Santees, Eastman went on to graduate with honors from Dartmouth (B.S.) and Boston University Medical School (M.D.). He wrote nine books and then re-entered Indian Service as inspector at Carlise. Dr. Eastman later investigated the Court Oreilles Reservation while Father Gordon was there.

Also attending Carlisle Institute was Jim Thorpe, named by the elders of his tribe "Athahuck" (Path-Lit-By-Lightning). He made the school famous for its football team and swept the track and field events at the 1912 Olympics, played professional baseball, and helped organize one of the earliest pro football teams. He was later the subject of controversy for his pro standing and was stripped of his Olympic medals.

While in the East, Father Gordon was often called upon to speak. The Baltimore *Sun*, reporting on the Federation of Catholic Societies Convention in 1914, said:

"The Indian priest, Rev. Philip Gordon of Superior, Wis., was also on the program. Father Gordon could not deny his Indian ancestry. Every line of his face revealed the red-skin, while his jet black hair added to the picture of the aborigines of America. However, imagine the surprise of the assembled delegates when Father Gordon entered into a most interesting discussion of the Indian missions in the most faultless English you could have heard. But what was even more striking than his unexpected pure English was his unusual wit, with which he kept his audience in almost continuous convulsions of laughter. He was a living proof of what real civilization has meant to the former wild tribes of our soil."

(Editor's Note: Father Gordon says he will take care of the Sun *when he comments on this hyperbole.)*

Father Gordon now began an active part in Indian affairs. He was impatient with the mismanagement and tactics of the bureaucracy that had been going on for so many years.

He knew the Indians generally were intelligent and perceptive and learned quickly. These were traits they had developed for generations, necessary for survival in their savage state. Unfortuately, for a hundred years they had been denied the kind of education they needed, largely because white teachers did not understand Indian ways and did not believe Indian children were capable of learning.

Segregated on reservations, the Indians developed a terrible feeling of hopelessness and despair. They needed someone to take an interest in their personal problems. Father Gordon always hoped he could help them. He was commended for his work at the Carlisle School by Monsignor William Ketcham, Director of the Bureau of Catholic Indian Missions. On March 6, 1915,

er Gordon beside the statue of St. Patrick in the church at Centuria, Wisconsin,
oto treasured by Paul Villaume.

WISCONSIN
OFFICIAL MARKER

PIERRE ESPRIT RADISSON
AND
MEDARD GROSEILLIERS

These brothers-in-law during the winter of 1659-60 camped with the Ottawa Indians two miles upstream from this point on Lac Court Oreilles (meaning "Lake of the Short Ears" in French). Early French explorers called the Ottawa Indians "Court Oreilles." Radisson's journal reports that among the gifts they brought to the Indians were "2 ivory combs and 2 wooden ones," also some "red paint and 6 looking glasses of tin." The combs and paint were "to make themselves beautiful, the looking glasses to admire themselves." Radisson and Groseilliers were the first white men to discover and explore northwestern Wisconsin. When the French Governor General of Canada confiscated their rich cargo of furs because he claimed they did not have the proper credentials to trade with the Indians, Radisson and Groseilliers left the service of the French government. They went to England and were instrumental in the formation of the Hudson's Bay Company in Canada.

Erected 1960
300th Anniversary
Discovery and Exploration of Northwestern Wisconsin

Father Gordon's grandparents, Mr. and Mrs. Antoine Gordon. Photo from Gordon Centennial booklet.

ernal grandparents of Father Gor-
Picture taken in 1890.

Father Gordon's father, Mr. William Gordon (left).

NAMEKAGON -
COURT OREILLES PORTAGE

Still visible here is the southeast terminus of the 2½ mile portage that linked the St. Croix and Chippewa River systems. Indians, explorers, missionaries and fur-traders all used this "carrying place" to move their birch bark canoes back and forth between the two great water routes connecting Lake Superior and the Mississippi. In 1784 Michel Cadotte established a fur-trading post at the northwest end of the portage to control the trade at this pivotal point. From such interior locations as Lac Court Oreilles the Chippewa Indians carried over here on their trips to the south and west to gather rice and berries and on their war excursions against the Sioux.

Erected 1956

rk-covered tepee like those Father Gordon's ancestors used. Replicas may be
en at Historyland, Hayward, Wisconsin.

toine Gordon's store. From a photo in **St. Croix Trail Country,** taken by the author,
G. Purcell, sometime before 1901.

BRULE-ST. CROIX PORTAGE

The Brule and St. Croix rivers provide the shortest natural water highway between Lake Superior and the Upper Mississippi. Daniel Greysolon, Sieur du Lhut, in 1680 was the first white man to use this passage.

Traveling from Prairie du Chien in 1766, Jonathan Carver was advised by his Chippewa guide not to ascend the Mississippi and St. Croix rivers because he lacked enough gifts for the numerous and unfriendly Sioux along that route. Carver's party then detoured up the Chippewa River to Lac Court Oreilles, portaged to the Namekagon, traveled down stream to the St. Croix and up that river to the passage north of St. Croix Lake.

The two-mile portage between the St. Croix and the Brule was used by another exploration party led by Henry Schoolcraft August 6, 1832. One of Schoolcraft's companions recorded that the Brule was a brook of clear, cold water "filled with brook trout." The Brule still is one of the best known trout streams in the United States.

Erected 1962

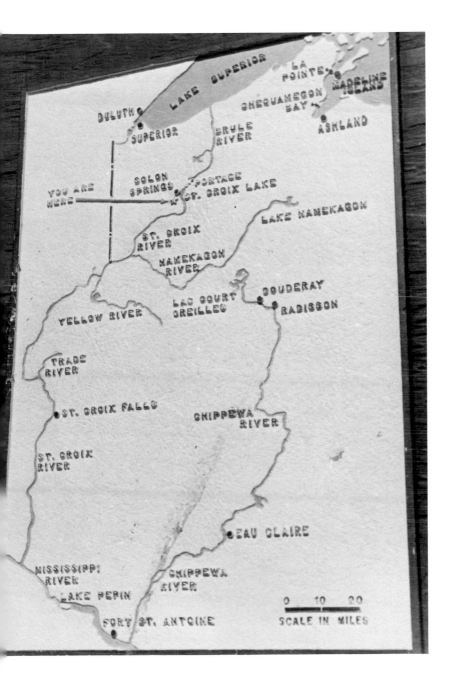

YELLOW RIVER

The Yellow River was called the "River Jaune" by early French explorers because of the bright yellow sand on the bottom of Yellow Lake through which it flows. Located in the heart of the "Folle Avoine," or wild rice country, it was one of the first tributaries of the St. Croix to be occupied by the Chippewa who (ca. 1700) in bloody battles drove out the Sioux and established permanent villages on Clam and Yellow Lakes.

At the beginning of the nineteenth century, rival fur-traders for the Northwestern and the XY Companies competed fiercely with rum, trade goods and credit for the fur-trade of the Yellow River, Namekagon, Clam and St. Croix bands of Chippewa Indians.

Indian mounds indicate the residences of aboriginal Indians (ca. 300 A.D.) along the Yellow River and on Spooner Lake, two miles northeast of here. Succeeding the Sioux, the Chippewa maintained permanent villages on this lake from the early eighteenth to the early twentieth century.

Erected 1968

The old church at Reserve, Wisconsin, which was destroyed by fire in 1921. From a postcard supplied by Trudy Wolf.

The new church of St. Francis Solano at Reserve, built by Father Gordon.

Saint Francis Solanus

THE SAINT ≈

Born in Spain in 1549.
Ordained a priest, in the Franciscan Order, age 27.
Left Spain for Peru in 1589.
Labored among the Indians of Peru as a missionary
for 20 years.
Died in the year 1610.
His Feast Day is on July 13.

THE MISSION ≈

The first converts about 1790 ~ fruits of the
exemplary Christian life of a certain _____
John Corbine, Frenchman.
1860-73 occasional visits by Missionary
Fathers from Bayfield.
Franciscan Fathers took charge in 1878.
Small log church begun in 1881 ~
completed and blessed in August 1885.
Same year ~ School and Sisters' Home
Church destroyed by lightning in 1921
Present building, made of native stone
1923-24
Sisters' new home 1936-37
New school erected 1941

Buckskin hanging in the church at Reserve, tanned by the Indians. Indian traditions were incorporated into the decorations of the church.

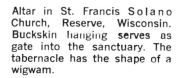

Altar in St. Francis Solano Church, Reserve, Wisconsin. Buckskin hanging serves as gate into the sanctuary. The tabernacle has the shape of a wigwam.

COURT OREILLES

The area around Lac Court Oreilles has long been a favorite habitat of Indians because of the abundant game, fish, berries and wild rice. Radisson and Groseilliers were the first white men to visit this area (1659) and they found Ottawa Indians. Before that the Sioux controlled this territory, and since 1745 the Ojibwa (Chippewa) Indians have lived here continuously. The Ottawa were called "Short Ears" by the French. Court Oreilles (Couderay) means "short ears." However, the Indians and early English and American explorers always referred to the area as Ottawa Sagaigan or Lake. The Court Oreilles Indian Reservation contains nearly 70,000 acres and was set aside by the Treaty of La Pointe in 1854. There are approximately 1500 Chippewa Indians living on the reservation at this time.

Erected 1955

Outdoor altar for the procession on the feast of Corpus Christi at Reserve, Wisconsin. The Indians celebrated the feast with a pageantry uniquely their own.

St. Patrick's Church at Centuria, Wisconsin, where Father Gordon served as pastor.

EARLY LOGGING INDUSTRY

In 1840 nearly one-sixth of the white pine west of the Appalachians grew here in the Valley of the Chippewa River. Containing some twenty-five billion board feet of virgin timber, this magnificent forest became an important basis of Wisconsin's first great industry. About 1840 it began to fall to the axes and saws of hardy woodsmen who swarmed westward principally from New England, Canada and the Scandinavian countries. Upper Chippewa drew from its tributaries, Moose, Couderay, Brunet, Thornapple, Flambeau and Jump Rivers. Feeding the sawmills of Chippewa Falls, Eau Claire, La Crosse and other river towns, it was distributed as lumber throughout the United States, an ingredient in the making of a great industrial nation. Early days motive power was oxen and river transportation.

Pine logging ended in 1905. Hardwood would not float; logging of same started in 1885, ended in 1945. Much sawed locally but several billion feet railed out after the railroad reached here in 1903. Rails entered Eau Claire in 1871, Ladysmith in 1885.

The rugged lumberjacks and rivermen who made this industry possible were contemptuous alike of hardship and danger. Such hazardous work as breaking log jams that formed in the rivers. One large jam at Chippewa Falls in 1869 which was fifteen miles long, thirty feet high in places and contained 150 million board feet. They gave freely of their energies and lives to change frontiers into settled communities. Their breed has not been seen in Wisconsin since the passing of large scale logging early in the twentieth century.

To their memory - and especially the 200 or more, many unknown, who died in carrying out their perilous labor - this marker has been erected by C. M. Olson, Couderay, in 1956. Also, the Tubby Forest Marker.

P.S. - Eleven men drowned when their bateau upset while breaking a log jam at Holcombe in 1905, the last big log drive on the old Chipp.

The "Chief," Father Gordon, visits his boys at Camp Grant, Illinois. "Photo Signal Corps, U. S. Army," furnished by Paul Villaume.

Pilgrims in Rome. Next to Father Gordon (wearing his Indian headdress), is Bishop Francis Kelly of Tulsa, Okla., and on his right Msgr. Buckey of Washington, D.C. In the third row, at the far right, is the present Cardinal John P. Cody of Chicago, who was then a young priest in the papal Secreteriat of State and serving as English interpreter for the Holy Father, Pope Pius XI.

Father Gordon, wearing his famous Indian head-dress.

Father Gordon and Al Smith at Notre Dame University.

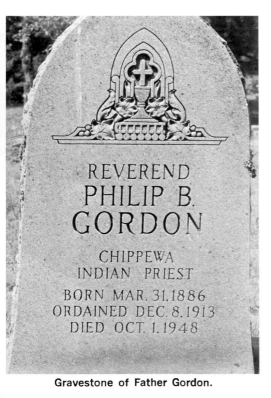

Gravestone of Father Gordon.

Gravestone of Antoine Gordon.

Monsignor Ketcham wrote to Bishop Koudelka of Superior:

"Rev. Philip Gordon, of the Diocese of Superior, will soon finish his course at the Mission House. The authorities of the Mission House tell me that he is equipped to do efficient missionary work, and I know that for sometime he has been putting in his Sundays at the Carlisle Indian School, where he has accomplished a great deal of good. We who are interested in the general work of the Indians believe that if we could employ him for a couple of years to do work in the large non-reservation government schools of the country that a great many Indian children would be saved to the Faith and an impetus given to our work in these institutions.

"I should be glad if Your Lordship would grant me permission to make use of Father Gordon for two years in the work I have mentioned."

Father Gordon had direct contact with the Federal Indian Bureau and the Catholic Bureau to which he was appointed in 1915. He observed the workings of Congress and met various members as well as Indian delegations. He joined the Society of American Indians, a group of educated Indians working for justice for the Redman and later became president of the organization.

The Indian priest knew the Indians needed more patience and understanding than they had been given and it was his earnest wish to spend his life helping them. His ideas did not always go well with church authorities. The Catholic Church, like the government, expected too many changes in too short a time.

Despite his criticism of Father Gordon's work, Bishop Koudelka was influenced by Ketcham's references and his request was granted. On March 25, 1915, Monsignor Ketcham wrote the following letter:

"Your favor of March 17, from Bridgeport, Conn., granting me permission to employ Father Gordon in the special work I have in mind for him, for a time, has been received. I beg to thank Your Lordship for your kindness in this regard.

"I am surprised at your remark, which seems to indicate that Father Gordon was not fulfilling his duties. It may be possible that in a matter of this kind the Indian disposition and character has to be taken into consideration. At any rate, Father Gordon will have a fair chance to do some very good work during the next two years, and this will give him a chance to 'prove his mettle'!"

Father Gordon worked strenuously with the Bureau of Catholic Indian Missions and became chairman of the advisory board of the Society of American Indians. He said it was a time of astonishing activity and violent agitation in behalf of the Indians. He traveled throughout many midwestern states as special missionary, covering Oklahoma, Nebraska, Kansas, the Dakotas, Michigan, and Minnesota. He attended many meetings and visited various government schools and private church institutions for Indians.

In the Kansas City *Star,* June 1, 1917, Father Gordon was called "a charming personality, highly educated and possesses a natural humor which makes his remarks very entertaining as well as interesting and instructive."

He spent some time in Kansas where he acted as chaplain to the Catholic Indian students at Haskell Institute, Lawrence, Kan. His outrage at conditions there led to an investigation of the school by government agencies and consequent dismissal of employees for religious discrimination and other irregularities.

His correspondence included caustic letters to high YMCA officials, government officials, and Congressmen. All this agitation caused uneasiness and dismay to the well-known Cardinal Gibbons, president of the Catholic Bureau. The Cardinal eventually asked Father Gordon to retire from the Bureau for the "good of the cause."

However, he received praise from the Director of the Bureau Wm. H. Ketcham in a letter to Bishop Koudelka of Superior, dated May 1, 1917:

"The Bureau of Catholic Indian Missions, in 1915, employed Rev. Philip B. Gordon for special work for a period of two years, an emergency salary having been secured for this specific purpose and period from an outside source.

"This action on the part of the Bureau was taken with your Lordship's permission, and, sometime later, on July 9, 1915, you formerly (sic) granted Father Gordon leave of absence from the Diocese of Superior for a period of two years from that date. Hence, while his engagement with the Bureau is up on June 1st, 1917, his leave of absence extends to July 9, of the same year.

"I have been instructed to notify Father Gordon that after June 1st, 1917, we cannot employ a priest for special work and that his connection with the Bureau will cease on that date. This notification will be sent immediately.

"I must thank your Lordship for allowing us the services of one of your priests for two years and will say that Father Gordon has worked diligently at the various tasks that have been given him to do. He is a young man of vast energy and possesses much talent. With the experience he has acquired he ought to be qualified to do very effective work in any diocese. I assure you we all wish him the greatest success possible in whatever work his superiors may assign to him."

Father Gordon knew many famous people on a first-name basis, but the extreme formality of address required by the church officials was a source of annoyance to him. In the column he later published in the *Inter-County Leader* at Frederic, he wrote, "In viewing the two previous articles, I see already I have stuck out my neck. For instance, I referred to the Bishop of the Diocese as 'the boss.' This is, according to Webster's Dictionary, 'Slang, U. S.' The correct reference to a Catholic Bishop is 'His Excellency, the Most Reverend So-and-So,' with a semi-pietistic bow in writing it. Such is the reverence and respect for authority expected of a priest."

Now that the time of his special assignment was completed, he again hoped that his cherished wish of being assigned an Indian parish would be achieved. But it was again delayed. The Indian priest was sent to collect money for an Orphan Home, an assignment he resented. A letter to his superior showed some bitterness at not being able to work among his people as he had always hoped and planned. This is shown in a letter which was addressed to the Franciscan missionary among the Chippewas, Father Chrysostom Verwyst:

"Dear Father Chrysostom: You had the kindness to send me a little book by Father Pierz sometime ago. I am going to ask you to allow me to retain this little book for a while longer. Just now, I am leaving for Washington and will probably be absent from the missions for two months or longer. Did you hear that I have been apopinted collector for our Orphan Home? This is not a very pleasant piece of work. Everybody is your critic and sometimes even holy men criticize very unjustly. For instance, I have already been called 'liar' 'abominable liar' etc. by my fellow-priests.

"I visited Nett Lake Reservation in northern Minnesota last week with Father Simon, O.S.B. Lots of pagans up there and no effort was ever made to convert them until Father Simon went up two years ago. Now a start has been made and much good may come out of it provided that the pagan Indians are not turned against Mother Church by too harsh methods of evangelization. Sometimes, the white priests are too strict with the Redman. They really expect too much from the neophytes. It took several hundred years to make good people out of the Germans and I know some who condemn the Indian because he is not a saint in a generation!!

"I discussed with Father Simon the question of my stay with the Chippewas for good. But dear Father, to the question: 'Why doesn't Father Gordon stay with the Chippewas', I must refer you to my Bishop. My Bishop is my superior and when the time comes for him to place me with the Chippewas, I suppose I shall be appointed. If I was my own 'boss' you may be sure I would have appointed myself to some Indian place a long time ago. I have frequently been advised by priests to stay with the Chippewas. Now you know how funny such a question sounds when one is working under orders of another.

"Were I to ask you: Stay with the Norwegians! or why don't

you stay with the Hollanders? you could rightfully retort, ask my Father Provincial! Some priests, strange to say, imagine that I travel about and work here and there *motu proprio*!! They don't seem to know that I am not an independent church by myself but am only one of a host of common laborers working under orders of Bishops.

"In your last letter you write: ' I hope you will stay — for good — with the Chippewas.' I hope so myself, dear Father. Would it not be proper for you to ask the Rt. Rev. Bishop this question? Then we would find out why our hopes are blasted."

After several months of attempting to collect for this cause, probably without much enthusiasm, Father Gordon wrote to the Bishop of Superior from White Earth, Minn., on October 17, 1917, admitting failure in this work and again appealing for an assignment to an Indian mission:

"You will not be surprised to hear that I did not have any success in my collecting-tour. I visited the cities of Kansas City, Chicago, Washington, Baltimore, Philadelphia and New York but could secure no audiences or having secured a hearing was repulsed.

"I am seriously thinking of resigning my position as your special collector. I have several opportunities to do missionary work among my own people. In the meantime, too, I hear that I have been slated for missionary work in our own Diocese. This may mean that I am again to become a *mere assistant to the Franciscans*, something which had already, I thought, proved unworkable.

"It seems to me that it would be both prudent and feasible to allow me to resume my former work of general missionary to the Indians. In that capacity, I am assured *a regular salary* as well as certain well-defined duties.

"While my leave of absence still allows me time to collect for your great Orphanage, I feel that my time is wasted if I attempt to collect just at this time. You know the demands on the public which rich Americans all feel must be placed ahead of all other appeals: Liberty Loan, Red Cross, K.C. & Y.M.C.A., Library, Belgian Relief, Polish Relief, etc., etc. It is possible that I may make another attempt to reach those who could help us by the thousands but this must be later.

"The Indians need me, dear Bishop, and you are not the one to allow the call of the Redman to go unheeded."

Correspondence followed between Father Gordon and the Bishop and friction developed, but harmony was restored by the following letter, written by the Apostolic Delegate, Archbishop John Bonzano, on December 15, 1917.

"Right Rev. Joseph M. Koudelka, D.D.
     "Bishop of Superior,
          "Superior, Wisconsin.

"Rt. Rev. and dear Bishop:

"The Rev. Philip Gordon called on me yesterday morning to explain to me the trouble which has arisen between himself and Your Lordship. He showed to me the telegram which was sent to him by your Secretary on October 26th directing him to take charge of the parish at Mellen, Wisc., the letter of Your Lordship, dated Nov. 2nd, in which you tell him to look for another Ordinary and give him thirty days' time to find one, and finally the *litterae excardinationis* which you gave to him for this purpose.

"The cause of his trouble which led up to his asking for an exeat and to Your Lordship's sending him the one which he displayed to me was, he asserts, his refusal to resume the work of collecting funds for your new orphanage. To justify this refusal he said that experience has taught him that, as an Indian, he is not capable of performing the work with much success among white people, and that, besides, he wishes to be employed in the Sacred Ministry for which he was raised to the priesthood. And, on my own account, I beg to observe that it does not seem to be an act of prudence to send around to collect a young priest who is ordained only four years. But, whatever may be said of the excuse given by the Rev. Father for his refusal to resume the work of collecting, I am sorry to remark, with reference to the *litterae excardinationis* given to him by Your Lordship, even though they were asked for by him, that, since they were not issued to the Ordinary of any particular Diocese nor were preceded by a written statement of any Bishop declaring himself willing to incardinate the Rev. Father, they are of no real canonical value.

"In consequence, therefore, since the Rev. Father had not nor has at present a serious intention of leaving the Diocese of Superior and only in a moment of anger, which in part is explicable, asked Your Lordship for an exeat, it follows that he continues to belong to the Diocese and that you cannot refuse to employ him but must give him an appointment as you previously did; and this the more so since the Diocese is in need of priest, as I have learned on other occasions.

"Awaiting an answer from Your Lordship telling me what you have done in the matter, I am, with sentiments of esteem and best wishes,

"Sincerely yours in Xt.,

"+ John Bonzano —
"Archbishop of Melitene
"Apostolic Delegate."

In January, 1918, during World War I, the Indian priest resumed his diocesan missionary work and volunteered as chaplain, awaiting appointment by the Ordinary of the U. S. Army and Navy Chaplains, the Most Reverend Patrick Hayes, D.D., later to become archbishop and then cardinal.

Father Gordon's appointment never materialized as the war ended soon after his appointment as pastor at Reserve and surrounding missions, where his long-time desire would come true, working among his people.

CHAPTER
XI
Mission at Reserve

FATHER GORDON'S ARRIVAL AT RESERVE WAS NOT ATTENDED BY any ceremony. One of his parish members, Katie Gohke, is still living there (in 1975). Katie is eighty-three now and a widow. She remembers the Indian priest well.

Katie says, "Father Gordon came to Stone Lake. That's where the Soo Line was. My husband was working in the store at Stone Lake. He came one day and asked if I could feed Father Gordon for dinner.

"I said, where is Father?"

"He's down to the store. I just want to know, will you give him dinner here?"

I said, "I'll feed him then."

So Katie gave Father Gordon his first meal at Reserve. She didn't remember what she served, probably roast beef. After that she was busy with her large family and did not have an opportunity to associate with the priest very much but she says everybody liked him.

Katie must have been very busy with thirteen children of her own, plus two children of relatives whom they raised. She has over a hundred grandchildren.

Other Indians at Reserve also remember Father Gordon.

Charlie Coons, who had a store and the postoffice, was not a Catholic, but he remembers Father Gordon and said he was a good man. Charlie's friend, Benny Isham, said he always went to church at Reserve and he liked the priest.

"He built the church there, but it wasn't finished when he left."

When Father Gordon came to Reserve, the church of St. Francis Solano, which the Franciscan missionaries had built many years before, was still standing. It was a log building begun in 1881, completed in 1885, and later enlarged.

The missionaries had converted several hundred Indians from paganism and two churches had been built on the Court Oreilles Reservation, one at Reserve and one at Post, as well as several outside the reservation, which were later given over to white Catholics.

By tribal action, the Indians had voluntarily given lands for the missions, and the Indians themselves furnished labor and materials for the churches.

The Most Rev. Joseph M. Koudelka had appointed Father Gordon missionary to the Chippewa Indians in January, 1918, at the suggestion of Cardinal Bonzano, Apostolic Delegate.

Among Indians living on the reservation, were Steve Grover (Go-Shens) Anakwat (The Cloud) and Billy Boy, pagan Indians who became good friends of Father Gordon. They were greatly respected for their age and wisdom. The orator of the band was Billy Boy who lived at Reserve and, as the priest said, was a master of the Chippewa language.

"It is a beautiful and sonorous language, full of original terms and lofty similies. There is as much difference between the common language of the reservation and that of the great orators as there is between the slang of our street Arabs and the literary idioms of our best writers."

It seemed logical to Father Gordon to be in charge of six Indian missions. Besides the one at Reserve, there were two on the Lac du Flambeau Reservation, one at Mud Lake in Rusk County, one at the mouth of the Yellow River, one at Old Post on the west branch of the Chippewa River.

As he later wrote in his memoirs, since he was "a Chippewa Indian, an enrolled member of the tribe, speaking the language, related by blood to many members of the tribe, reared with the Indians in their own haunts, the appointment seemed fitting and in keeping with the idea of a native clergy for the aborigines of the country."

He believed he was where he belonged and felt he was conducting his work successfully. But it was not long before a government investigation took place. Father Gordon was annoyed and unhappy about the report from Commissioner Cato Sells. On April 5, 1920, he sent the following telegram to the Hon. Joseph P. Tumulty, President Wilson's secretary, and also sent a copy to the bishop at Superior.

"In report just received from Commissioner Cato Sells an investigation recently conducted in Courte Oreille Reservation, reported by Inspector Lipps in a most unfair and unjust way. Unless the President directs within forty-eight hours a reinvestigation to take place within the next ten days which must be based on fact and reliable data instead of uncatholic prejudice and malicious anti-catholic bigotry and gross allegations I must call the attention of the whole Catholic hierarchy to this rabid anticatholic proceedings and by pen and voice tell twenty-nine million Catholics and upright Americans of our country of this unfair, unjust, unAmerican and decidedly anti-catholic piece of administration; also an apology is due us from Inspector Lipps for his trying statements and misrepresentations. Wire me at once Hayward, Wisconsin."

Father Gordon's good friend, Senator Lenroot, wrote to Cato Sells on June 5, 1918, "I wish to state in this connection that Father Gordon can be absolutely relied upon in every respect and that he is the greatest power for good that there has been among the Indians since I have been in Congress, which is now nearly ten years.

"He is an Indian himself, and a Catholic priest of the very highest ideals, of absolute integrity and full of enthusiasm for the welfare of the Indians . . . and in matters concerning this reservation you will find him of very great value in giving to the Department disinterested information concerning the various problems that arise."

Father Gordon not only cared for his six missions, but he visited the Potawatomi Indians of eastern Wisconsin, who had long been neglected by the government and missionaries. Dr. Carlos Montezuma, a noted Chicago physician, accompanied him to the Potawatomi reservation, where they discussed plans for a mission.

Dr. Montezuma was a full-blooded Apache, a fluent writer and speaker and a 33rd degree Mason. He wore his hair quite long and for this reason he has a namesake still living at Reserve. When "Monty" Diamong was born he had unusually long hair. Father Gordon said, "Here is a second Montezuma" and that was the name he received.

Among other well-known guests the priest entertained was Eamon de Valera, who became prime minister of Ireland. He was honored by the Indians and received an Indian name. In return De Valera presented a number of rifles to the Indians. These were treasured by the Indians, and no doubt at least some of them are still being used.

When De Valera died on August 29, 1975, at the age of 90, a St. Paul paper mentioned the fact that he was an Indian chief.

Father Gordon encountered further trouble. In 1921 the old church burned. Katie Gohke saw it burn. She says, "Father Gordon was away at the time. The steeple got struck by lightning and then it went right down into the church. It was about 11 or 12 o'clock. I think part of it was a log building. It was a big, long building."

The Indian priest now faced the tremendous task of building a new church in a parish where "a dollar looked like a thousand." He personally collected $30,000 from friends of the Indians.

Clarence Wise, banker of Hayward, financed large loans on unsecured personal notes. Later, his son, Tony, did much to help the Indians.

Father Gordon dreamed of a church that would combine the old Indian symbolism and the ideals of Catholicism. He said this would be a "connecting link which would sagely bring Indians from paganism to Catholicism . . . it is the only way to reach the Indian's heart."

The Indians were enthusiastic about the new church. They picked up granite rock from the fields and woods of Reserve, carried them to the building site and split them. It was slow work and the roof was covered with building paper until it could be completed. Father Gordon planned to use rough cedar shingles, called "shakes" for the roof. These were to be hand-hewn from immense stumps that stood beside the lake on which Reserve was located.

The priest's many friends were always ready to help. Alexander C. Eschweiler, Milwaukee architect, planned the building but the head carpenter and two masons were Indians.

A newspaper article describing the church said, ". . . Indian psychology has been taken into consideration in working out the symbolic designs of the stained glass windows by George W. Mueller of the Milwaukee Mirror and Art Glass Works. Realizing that few of the Indian parishioners were able to read, Mr. Mueller planned the windows so that each shall speak to the Indians in familiar terms. They contain the rising sun, many arrows, crossed calumets and tobacco, and above the pipes and arrows, the cross."

The hand-hewn rafters in the interior of the church were stained in brilliant reds and blues and orange which the Indians loved. Deerskins hung in front of the confessionals and at the entrance to the altar. The altar cloths were woven by the Chippewa women with characteristic designs and Indian symbols woven into the fabric.

Adjoining the church was the pastor's residence, built in the shape of a teepee, the pointed wigwam of the early Indians. This had a lighting system and a bath with hot and cold water — unheard-of marvels among the Indians.

All during the building process, Father Gordon was available to help in any part of the construction. The architects, the window designers, or anyone doing any work in connection with the building, sought his advice in interpreting Indian symbols and suggesting ways in which they could be combined with Catholic teaching.

The roof of the church was not finished when Father Gordon was transferred and it saddened him to think the beautiful church as well as the Indians' souls were being neglected.

"Yes, my people are dirty, looked at through white men's eyes," Father Gordon said. "But they have no training or facilities for being otherwise. Thirty-five percent of them are affected with tuberculosis and they know nothing of how to stop its ravages."

But he was justly proud of the seventy boys under his care who volunteered for service in France, seven of whom gave their lives for a cause which they understood only dimly but which they believed was just because the good priest said it was.

"I never want to leave Reserve," he said. "This is the work I love and understand and I ask as my only reward greater appreciation on the part of the white men of the Indians' problems. Oh, I might want to go to Chicago once in a while to see Babe Ruth play baseball, but I hope to live and die among my people."

In spite of all the poverty and sickness, however, the Indians loved to dance and would continue for weeks if not restrained. The priest's father was quite modern in his ideas, but his Indian mother loved the old ways and appeared on ceremonial occasions in full regalia.

The year 1923 was disastrous for Father Gordon. It is notable for the destruction of the parish at Post when the Chippewa Flowage project was completed. Father Gordon later wrote: "In 1923, the Northern States Power Company, a powerful corporation, rendered useless the other mission church located at Post,

Wis., by reason of the construction of a reservoir which flooded the Catholic mission grounds and inundated some 250 Catholic graves. The writer engaged at once with his characteristic vigor and vigilance and almost overheated vim in correspondence and controversy with the Indian Department officials at Washington, D. C. under whose permission the reservoir was constructed and with officials of the Water Power Company; and endeavored in vain to interest the Bishop of Superior in whose name the church property lies, in the matter of proper redress for the poor Indians as well as damages and respect for the sanctity of Catholic graves and church."

A controversy had been going on for years between the Indians and the company officials. But eventually, Indians were obliged to give up their old homes. Indian graves, sacred to them, were flooded, the Indian church abandoned and the Indians were grieved and puzzled.

Father Gordon wrote, "Naturally, the Indian pastor was in the midst of this fight sticking out his neck many times publicly and privately. A voluminous correspondence is evidence of the tremendous efforts he made in behalf of the Indians.

"Here, too, and naturally, the disfavor of the public utilities with their corps of attorneys, officials, lobbyists, etc. associated therewith, was incurred. Still, many new friends were made and thus the disagreement raged."

As an example of the repercussions of such an event, the priest said, "I was asked to address a district convention of the Women's Clubs who were meeting in St. Croix Falls. We took the occasion to ask the women as good citizens to ask for a complete U. S. Senate investigation of the whole Chippewa Flowage project."

Father Gordon had difficulty continuing his talk because of opposition from the floor, and just managed to read his resolution (which the meeting subsequently adopted).

He said, "Following his appearance, the speaker was soundly berated by two of the members of the convention (females). Later he discovered that the two good women were employees of the Public Utilities at Eau Claire, Wis. He was accused of obstructing 'progress' and civilization.' "

Early in 1923, Father Gordon had been appointed to the Secretary Work's Committee on Indian Affairs, a committee of one hundred Americans who were asked to come to Washington to formulate an Indian policy. The committee was directed to meet in December.

The meeting brought together a rather unique group of Americans — Gen. Pershing, Rabbi Stephan Wise, Mary Roberts Rinehart, the authoress, Oswald Willard, Maj. Gen. Hugh Scott, William Jennings Bryan, Nicholas Murray Butler, Bernard Baruch, Gov. Preuss of Minnesota, Dr. Charles Eastman, and others.

According to Father Gordon, "The activities caused the Indian Bureau some worry and efforts were initiated to silence the voices crying for justice. Indians were instigated to complain, allegations arose, were reported, refuted, 'investigations' made."

At this time, Father Gordon wrote a paragraph for the Superior *Telegram,* which was copied by the Notre Dame University Bulletin and many Catholic and secular newspapers.

He wrote, "It is an old trick of the Indian Office to blacken the character of any Indian that happens, notwithstanding the retardation caused by the Indian Bureau, to rise a little above the ranks. So as soon as an educated Indian begins to deplore the conditions of his brother Indians, the Indian Office dubs such a one as a disturber, an agitator, and lately he is placed in the Bolshevik class. The whole Indian Bureau system of managing Indian business to the detriment of the Indian but for the benefit of a few greedy and voracious whites, is the most dramatic autocracy in existence the world over. Gradually through assistance of the American press, the generous-hearted and justice-loving American people are learning something of this present day Indian government humbuggery and deceit practiced by the Indian Office forces."

He went on to tell of the plight of the Indians, but his pleas were to no avail. Father Gordon was finally retired from Indian missionary work. The relentless destiny of the Indian could not be reversed.

In September of the same year, 1923, the last meeting of the Society of American Indians took place in Chicago. Father Gordon had been elected president of the organization. The society was violently anti-Indian Bureau. They criticized the bureau severely and called on the American people for its total abolishment. Naturally, the activities of the group aroused the ire of many government officials who were working in the Indian office.

But the event which Father Gordon thought brought events to a climax came in November, 1923. The newly elected U. S. Senator Henrik Shipstead of Minnesota toured the northern part of his state. He visited the Chippewa Indians. On his return he asked Father Gordon to meet with him and talk over Indian matters. They met in the Radisson Hotel in Minneapolis, Minn. The priest said, "Outside of a picture in the newspaper, not much resulted except that the Senator was shown to be a fine friend of the Indians."

However, only two months later, early in January, 1924, Father Gordon received an urgent call from an old missionary at White Earth, Minn., Benedictine Father Aloysius, who had been with the Indians for forty years. He asked Father Gordon to come up at once and make a private survey of the deplorable conditions prevailing among the Indians.

Father Gordon responded immediately and after a week's visit, returned to the Twin Cities with a briefcase full of accounts of extreme distress and near starvation.

He presented the facts to Clubs, particularly the Catholic Women's Clubs in session in Minneapolis. He also contacted Governor Preus and other state officials and even stirred the American Red Cross to some activity in behalf of the Indians in Minnesota.

"Naturally," he said, "the Indian Office was severely taken to task and a controversy raged, the writer himself not being spared.

He was characterized as an agitator, a demagogue, and a dangerous character."

Despite a multitude of friends, there were factions who opposed the Indian priest. Interests he had opposed began a bitter campaign against him, even using some of his own people against him. Although he had staunch friends, "the shadow of amazing and overwhelming duplicity of government inspectors and employees often darkened the sun."

He described the termination of his stay at Reserve as follows:

"Meanwhile, in September, 1923, some disffected Indians, mostly non-Catholic, led by a renegade Indian who had served a term in State prison and aided and abetted by certain government agencies, . . . filed absurd and ridiculous charges affecting the personal conduct of the writer. The subsequent 'investigation' of the government officials disclosed nothing and the Bishop himself conducted and undertook a secret inquiry . . . the complainants publicly known to be irresponsible and even immoral. Two of the complainants have now admitted by affidavit that the matter was the characteristic American 'frame-up.' "

Father Gordon "secured the services of a reputable lawyer, Mr. Felix Streckymans, 640 Burnham Building, Chicago, Ill., who carefully went over the complete charges, (Note: All of the charges were not known to us until three years later) found nothing criminal among the allegations and nothing substantiated unless the poor judgment, too willing to be admitted by the writer, he considered worthy of a charge. Mr. Steckymans made several visits to the Reserve home of the missionary, conferred with numerous Indians and whites, including several of the actual complainants and reached the conclusion that the charges were so indefinite as to be ridiculous and were false. He so informed Bishop Pinten."

The following January, 1924, the Right Reverend Pinten asked Father Gordon to resign his Indian mission at Reserve, "for administrative reasons, advancing no other reason except to say, 'you will be sorry' . . . finally threatening."

Thus Father Gordon ended his work at Reserve, as he says, "without controversy and without complaint and without bitterness."

He returned to other areas of Indian work and in May, 1924, he was appointed pastor of St. Patrick's Church, Centuria, Wis. It was "a period of unforgettable memories, of total disillusionment, of anguish of friends."

Father Gordon had been informed that four delegations of Indians called on the bishop and six or seven hundred signed a pathetic petition. But their plea to "Come back, our son, come back," was ignored by the authorities. (The priest believed the number of delegations was exaggerated and possibly two would be closer to the truth.)

CHAPTER
XII
The Budding of an Orator

~~~~~~

"BUSINESS AS USUAL DESCRIBES THE COMING OF A NEW pastor," Father Gordon wrote in his column in the *Inter-County Leader*, at Frederic, Wis. However, two weeks after his arrival, on May 26, he wrote, "something most significant of the feelings of the real Catholic heart took place in the rectory. The occasion was the feast of Philip Neri. There were gathered a few of the families who came to wish the new pastor a 'Happy Namesday.' While the good people missed the day by a few weeks, since we are named after St. Philip, the Apostle, May 1, instead of Philip Neri, nevertheless the little gathering will be long re membered.

"Someone had written a poem, a spiritual bouquet was presented and lunch was served. All departed conscious of having performed a good deed. The pastor thanked God that he was in the midst of a devout Catholic people."

Centuria was located in a predominantly Scandinavian community, but the parish to which Father Gordon was assigned was mainly Irish, with some German and French, but no Indians. There were some Indian families in the area but they were not active members of the parish.

79

When Father Gordon arrived, the church and parish house were at Long Lake, about four miles from the village. They had been built on six acres of land donated by Lawrence Williams and Edward Kelley.

There are a number of people in the area who in 1975 still remember the Indian priest. They all loved Father Gordon.

Charlie Turner, 77, has farmed on the shores of the lake for many years. He was treasurer of the Long Lake Church during Father Gordon's time. The official name of the parish was St. Patrick's, but it was generally known as Long Lake Church.

Charlie says, "The church used to be right up here. If you go up to Sinon Lynch's, you go right by the cemetery. That's where the church and the priest's house originally were. The first church was built for $218.00. That burned and they rebuilt it. Then they moved it into Balsam Lake. It's on the west side of Balsam Lake. It's a real nice church yet."

Charlie loves to visit and went on philosophizing about the Indians.

"You know Indians aren't very thrifty. They do today and let tomorrow take care of itself. They don't worry about tomorrow. And they can't drink. That's their downfall. They had no booze before the white man came. But Father Gordon never drank. Or his father, Will Gordon. He stayed with Father for a while. I knew him, too, and he said he had a brother that drank.

"One day Will Gordon's mother was crying" he told me, "and he asked what was the matter. She said her son was drinking again. He knelt down by her chair and told her, 'Mother, you don't need to worry about me because I'll never take a drink.' And I knew him and we had him to the house for many meals, served wine, he wouldn't touch it. Nuthin'. Not even wine."

Charlie said Father Gordon would go into a tavern and drink a short beer. "I knew him real good. I think he done it to be friendly. Everybody liked him and I never in my life knew anybody say anything agin' him. I never could see that he was checking. He might have been. But everybody was friendly and

I know he didn't consider himself any better than anybody else."
When Father Gordon checked the records of his predecessors
at St. Patrick's he found many interesting entries. The financial
accounts written by Father Wirz in his "Parish Account Book"
detailed every cent taken in and disbursed. Father Gordon decided
"he was not a trained bookkeeper. His arithmetic seems to be
correct and if not correct, the records were kept straight by
various notations, generally in red ink. Here is one:
 " 'N. B. Till January 1st, 1880, this mission was taxed (or
better this mission taxed itself) $75.00 a year. From the 1st day
of January, 1880, I taxed this mission only 45 dollars. A collection
of oats every year included. Also some contributions I should
get for my horse, buggy, etc.'
"A little later, on the same page: '1884, Aug. 23. I make a
present of the half for having kept horse, buggy, etc. (as above.)
$131.35 ÷ 2 = $65.62.'
"Father Wirz has recorded on many pages of his Parish Account Book his various lists of contributions and on an opposite
page his list of disbursements in the construction of the church
that replaced the old original log church. It is really remarkable
the number of five dollar donations listed. These contributions
were continuous beginning about 1873. The church construction
apparently took several years as disbursements indicate carpenter
bills and lumber bills up into the year 1883. In fact, Father Duren
who was to follow Father Wirz will tell us that the church was
only partially completed when he took charge in 1884.
"Among the sources of revenue listed by Father Wirz, there
are several put down as "By a kind of Festival." One dated
July 4th, 1873 netted $96.12. The following year, the 4th of July
"Festival" took in $141.60. I notice this item: 'For Keg of Beer,
$2.80.' "
Father Wirz' record of the original contract for constructing
the church is interesting in comparison to present day building
contracts.
"1875 Aug. 29. Gave the church of Long Lake to H. M. Lillis

to build it according to agreement between him, the Trustees and the Priest. To frame it according to the priest's direction for the sum of $215.00."

He then gave the size of the door and window openings in two more lines. . . . Later on, the same year, the agreement was amended by the addition of these words: "I agreed with Henry Lillis to pay him $15.00 for extra work. He has to build an altar, too; and moreover, he has to make some kind of pews into it; he has to make pews only when he has somebody from the congregation to help him." It seems the altar and pews were an afterthought.

Another of Father Wirz' N.B.'s: "Oct. 24, 1877, Henry Lillis said he would be satisfied with $30 and give the other $15 towards the church."

The final balancing Father Wirz has in bright red ink. "Dr. $554.84. Cr. $554.84. N. B. The above accounts were very carefully examined by Emma Connolly, Michael Williams, (Trustee) (partially only) and by me. But should there be nevertheless any error, I am willing to answer for the correction.

"Long Lake, Milltown, Polk County, Wisconsin, United States, America, on Saturday, this 23rd day of August, A. D. 1884. Henry Joseph Wirz, Old Pastor. L.D.A.Q.M." The concluding initials could not be interpreted by Father Gordon.

Beginning in 1926 services were held in Centuria in the old Murphy Store Building and Town Hall until the parish bought the property where the church was built.

The priest's arrival in Centuria began another active period in his life. He had the task of again collecting money for a church. The first assessment for the new chapel was declared to be ten loads of rock and the rock pit on the Hurley farm was designated as having rocks of the desired size. "Rocks the size of a baseball to as big as one can lift were acceptable."

Father Gordon had a different set of problems in his new parish, in a Protestant community. He wrote, "It was evident from the attitude of some of my brothers of the cloth that opposition to the Catholic Church was a necessary evil and bound to exist. I do not believe the clergy was agreed on any plan to fight on this particular one of the four freedoms. My own particular and definite way was to initiate a series of lectures. I always believed that a great deal of the antipathy to anything even remotely Catholic, was due in large part to sheer ignorance.

"The whole series of lectures was meant to meet the stereotyped objections hurled against the Catholic Church ever since the founding of the Republic in 1776."

It is hard to believe now that such lack of communication existed between the various religions. There seemed to be a fear that the Pope interfered with American politics, in fact, that there was a contest as to who was going to rule the country, the President or the Pope.

Charlie Turner relates, "You know it was rough. We had Protestants all around us. And they got some of the craziest ideas, just crazy ideas. You know I hired a fellow from Turtle Lake and he was here about three weeks and one Sunday morning we was gettin' ready to go to church and he says, 'Do you care if I go to church with you?'

"And boy, you know he sat there and he watched every move and after Mass he says to me, 'Could I see the basement?'

"Well," I says, "we just finished puttin' the basement under the church. There ain't nuthin' in there." But Charlie showed him the basement. Later the man admitted he saw nothing out of the ordinary in the church. He told Charlie, "The stories they told me was the basement was full of rifles and the Catholics were going to take the country over.

"Such damn crazy things and he actually believed it."

There are people who still remember the lectures. Mrs. Marie Mulvaney Hersant, formerly of Hudson, knew Father Gordon personally.

"I was fourteen or fifteen years old and my family would be in Balsam Lake on vacation. We attended Mass at St. Patrick's in Centuria. He always had a message."

Mrs. Edith Anderson, one of the Swedes from Route 1, Frederic, says, "Father Gordon was a hero of mine from the days when I worked in Centuria and he was an active local and national figure. We always exchanged greetings and I listened and read everything available. If anyone had charisma, he did." Scipio Wise, Hayward, also spoke of the Indian priest's charisma.

Louis de Angelo was a member of St. Patrick's for many years, and remembered the lectures.

"We got pretty well acquainted, He and I had a lot in common as far as politics are concerned. He was a good speaker and he devoted his life to charity, I might say. It made no difference if he had a dollar or not, he was just as happy.

"He really spent his life for the good of humanity, for the Indians especially. I know he made a lot of trips to Washington and to Madison and did a lot of things for the Indians that an ordinary person wouldn't have done. He was ahead of his time in his efforts to convert the Indians. The church was more straight-laced at that time."

There were also many, many non-Catholics who attended the lectures. A well-known artist from St. Paul, commented, "A systematic hearing of these lectures is a liberal education."

Father Gordon did much to erase the differences between the religious and ethnic groups. He was everybody's friend and had always been broad-minded. He said, of his lectures, "It is certainly not intended to prove that the Catholic religion is better (or as good or worse) than any Protestant denomination, nor is it proposed to indicate that the Catholic method is everywhere and always the best. As a matter of fact, I believe if I were Pope, I might make a change here or there. And if I happened to be the immediate local boss (the Bishop) I might add some new rules or abolish some old ones."

One of the things he probably would have changed was the matter of parish boundaries. In a preliminary statement to his published parish history, when he explained how the Catholic Church was governed, he suggested that people "Clip these items and preserve them in a scrap book for reference in future days. Perhaps the day may come when this country will no longer be a Democracy but will have some alien method of government thrust upon it. When that day arrives (which God forbid!) we might take up our scrap book and as a matter of historical interest read these poorly written, hasty articles to find out how the Catholic Church was run way back in those days when the great American people were fed plenty of lusty alphabetical soup all the way from AAA, and CCC to XYG and BUNK."

The Indian priest not only preached ecumenism. He was a shining example in his actions. The postmaster and his wife, in the village of Luck, were Theosophists, which is an Asian Indian religion. They believe if there is a life hereafter, you come back as something else and they do not believe in Christ as Christians do.

These people lived in the rear of the Post Office, which was common in a small town in those days. Every year at Christmastime, they would put a picture of the Christ Child in the window. They didn't believe in Christ, but they did this for their friends who were Catholic, Lutheran, Methodist. It was their way of saying Merry Christmas.

One night in the middle of winter, Father Gordon got a call from the postmaster, "Please come right over." Father Gordon asked what was wrong and he said his wife was sick. Father Gordon traveled through the snow and found that the wife was not sick, she was dead. The man had been sitting with his wife's remains for a number of hours. Where was he to turn? He went to an Indian priest.

Father Gordon said, "What have you done about this?"

"What can I do?"

"Well, you're going to have to get a doctor to certify that your wife died of natural causes and you're going to have to get her buried."

Father Gordon called the undertaker and arranged for the funeral. He conducted the funeral at the graveside, using the

King James' version of the Bible. He was criticized for doing it and some said they were going to write to the Bishop.

Father Gordon said, "I will be glad to give you his address."

His liberalism was indicated again when he paid tribute to Chief Kahquados of the Potawatomi tribe. "He was quite typical of the old-fashioned Indian. I don't mean he was a savage, but he always exemplified that type of manhood that believes in honesty and true attachment to ideals, even though these ideals may not have been learned in a Christian Church. . . . He often expressed sadness because of the trend of affairs that concerned the Potawatomi Tribe. He lived in poverty himself and he told me more than once that he did not mind penury but he suffered much to see the Potawatomi children endure hardship which he thought should have been prevented by the Great White Father."

Father Gordon was concerned about the state of morality throughout the country. "As Catholic pastor in charge of activities and spiritual life, the whole territory is of concern to us. Wherever a healthy religious spirit prevails there will reign community peace and concern, mutual charity, and respect for lawful authorities.

"Hence, our anxiety as we witness decline of religion and increase of religious indifference. Religion has truly fallen into descent. At least 70% of our people do not attend church. As an American citizen by reason of my ancestry we bear in mind the old philosophic maxim repeated by George Washington in his farewell address: 'Of all the dispositions and habits that will lead to politcal prosperity, religion and morality are indispensable supports.' "

On December 27, 1925, "A musicale was substituted for the regular lecture. Prof. Clarence Dickopf of St. Thomas College, St. Paul, entertained with a program of selections on the pianoforte and explained each piece before he played. He gave parts from the works of such Catholic composers as Grieg, Liszt, Chopin, Beethoven, Schumann and Palestrina. Assisting in instrumental selections were Helen Reidner, Dorothy Thill, Lenore

Lynch and Edna Towers. Joe Cloutier sang Ave Maria. The program was a benefit for the vaguely contemplated new Chapel for Centuria."

Plans for the chapel developed and on December 7, 1929, Father Gordon wrote to Rev. Eugene J. McGuinness, Vice-president & General Secretary, Catholic Church Extension Society: "It is our plan to construct a little Chapel in the village of Centuria which is the Post Office point of our rural St. Patrick's Church. To date the 26 struggling Catholic families in the village have gathered sufficient funds to buy twelve fine village lots and have about $300 in cash in hand besides. We hope to raise about $1500 by subscription. We do not propose to incur any debt. It would seem, therefore, that we will need your kind assistance to the extent of $1,000 at least   "

A small church was built in Centuria, which was later enlarged.

CHAPTER
XIII
Father G. and the KKK

FATHER GORDON'S SERIES OF LECTURES WERE INITIATED TO offset some of the specific items of complaints against the Catholic Church which were asserted by purposely ill-informed and anti-Catholic talkers touring the country and very active in neighboring counties.

One man especially, called Pat Malone, was particularly active in Barron and Rusk Counties. The C. F. Schmit Council No. 2137 of Rice Lake, Wis., instituted an investigation and reported: Malone was a Klan speaker spewing forth his rottenness . . . going about shooting hot air and running bills he never paid . . . getting into a bad scrape at Neillsville, involving the wife of a citizen there . . . an inmate for a time at the home of the notorious Kruegers, who killed United States officers after resisting the government draft . . . not an ex-priest as advertised . . . very crude . . . the kind of 100% un-American trash that is out traducing the loyal Catholics of this country and attempting to remove the First, Second, Fourteenth and Fifteenth Amendments from the Constitution."

From Ladysmith in Rusk County, under date of April 22, 1926, a letter to Father Gordon stated, ". . . The class of people supporting 'Pat Malone' were either supremely ignorant or bigoted. The intelligent and the business men realized that he was a professional mud-slinger, out to wrest the people of their hard-earned money through his malicious fanaticism. The latter considered him quite a joke. Pat Malone was abetted by one minister only in Ladysmith, the Rev. Sawyer, a Christian minister. The others, particularly the Methodist and Congregational ministers were heartily and militantly against him. These latter were even challenged by 'Pat' to debate but refused to have anything to do with the fanatic.

"This Malone has residence in Milwaukee. His real name is Arthur Malone; he formerly made a living as a partner of a young doctor who performed illegal operations somewhere in Wisconsin . . . It would do my heart good, and I would feel avenged, if a bunch of sturdy young lads would give him the fine ducking and a forceful egress from your town.

"(Signed) L. J. Quigley, O.S.M."

Around the beginning of May, 1926, a fiery cross was seen blazing near the Ed Murphy and Dennis Murphy farms. It was taken as a sort of challenge by some of the Irish farmers and some feeling was aroused, particularly against the County Sheriff.

Some suggested that Father Gordon ought to write or telegraph the governor, John J. Blaine. He followed the suggestion and on May 11, 1926, the governor wrote to Mr. George B. Mattson, Sheriff of Polk County, Balsam Lake. Dear Sir: "Complaint has been filed that one of your deputy sheriffs was implicated in the burning of a cross in connection with some meeting of the Ku Klux Klan.

"The burning of the cross is very offensive to a large group of our people, even to a large group who are not members of any church, the feeling being that it is a desecration of the very sacred symbolism of civilization. Due to such feeling and due to the fact that the Klan is an organization of hates and haters, the assemblage of a large number of people under such circumstances, in such a demonstration, has a tendency to incite a breach of the peace and disorder. In fact, such meetings often incite a breach of the peace.

"I think it would be just cause for removal if a sheriff of this state participated in any such demonstrations, especially when it is the duty of the sheriff to hold himself in readiness to prevent any breach of the peace.

"Therefore, if one of your deputies participated in one of these demonstrations, he should be removed at once. . . ."

Sheriff Mattson replied on May 14 stating that if any of his deputies were guilty of committing an unlawful act he would be removed from office at once. He listed his regular deputies who received a salary as: James Ely, Undersheriff, Chris Peterson, Deputy, Louis Soderberg, Deputy, Harry Mattson, Deputy, and Albert E. Mattson, Special Deputy, as well as several who served without pay.

On April 26, 1926, August E. Ender, editor of the Rice Lake *Chronotype,* Rice Lake, Wis., replied to Father Gordon's letter, saying, ". . . as to the class of people who visited and supported Pat Malone, the city of Chetek will furnish perhaps the best example. That city is over 95 percent non-Catholic and as being more or less opposed at all times to the Catholic religion. Well, the upshot of the meetings was that at a mass meeting held at the school, it was resolved by the Parent-Teachers Association that all would stay away from the meetings, and that they would try to keep their children away also, especially from meetings for men and women only . . .

"At Barron the leading KKK among the business men, owner of a general store, incurred the displeasure of Lutherans, Episcopalians and members of the Masonic order and others to such an extent that he has sold out. None of the ministers of Barron supported Pat Malone, but nearly all actively opposed him, and he was forbidden the use of the Methodist church, and Rev. Clark of the Baptist Church said his utterances were 'un-Christian.' Pat finally set up shop in a big tent, and ridiculed all of the ministers in Barron.

"Reports that came from Ladysmith say the last meeting was a joke, and God in his infinite mercy may have seen fit to send Pat there because since then the Masons and Knights of Columbus have often been honored guests of each other at invited meetings, and the value of the free advertising to the Catholic Church is too great to be measured in dollars and cents. Pat said the Methodist minister at Ladysmith, Rev. T. Harry Kelley, was a Romanist in disguise, and Kelley came back at him and silenced him for good in that community.

"You have been doing a noble work in educating the people as to the aims of Malone's panhandling tactics. He is always looking for trouble and to put enough kick into his meetings he usually has to jump onto some unoffending Protestants.

"Cordially, A. F. Ender"

In 1941, Father Gordon was to reminisce about the affair, "After fifteen years and knowing the people of the county better than in those days, I often wonder if all the perturbation was worth the while or was necessary. In later years, I even came to think that someone of the Irish themselves might have burned a cross 'to get Murphy mad.' "

But, he said, "the letters will indicate how degenerate become the workings of an organization such as the Ku Klux Klan, built on racial and religious prejudice. I often wonder if the set of men and women who do so much criticizing of any anti-Semitic utterances in these days and are willing to bar Father Coughlin from the air, because of alleged anti-Jewish sentiments felt the same when their Catholic fellow-citizens and Catholic neighbors were under fire from the likes of the creature known as 'Pat Malone.' "

Pat Malone apparently left the scene. Most Catholics were not particularly aroused. Some members of the American Legion urged some action, but there was really nothing that could be done and so the event passed into history.

However, in 1941, Father Gordon wrote, "One of the most remarkable coincidences that I have ever noted was to read the following news clipping taken from the Minneapolis Star-Journal issue of August 9, 1941:

"PAT MALONE WILL GIVE TWO TALKS

"Evangelist Pat Malone, guest speaker, will deliver another of his series of sermons at Prospect Park Baptist Church Sunday. He concludes his series the following week.

"Malone's morning sermon topic, 'The One Besetting Sin,' will follow morning worship at 11 a.m.

" 'The Greatest Tragedy Ever Recorded' will be his evening topic and follows prayer service at 7:30."

Father Gordon thought it would be worth a great deal if someone undertook to satisfy his curiosity and find out if this Pat Malone, Evangelist, is by any means the same Pat who had stirred up the community fifteen years earlier.

"Maybe (as I sincerely hope) the resemblance of names is purely accidental. Two men can easily have the same name in this vast country of ours. If by chance, it is the same Malone, then God help those Baptists!"

Father Gordon felt progress had been made in at least one area when he quoted a write-up of what he called one of the most unique events in which he had been involved:

"Perhaps the committee in charge unwittingly arranged it so, or perhaps they did it deliberately but Centuria Commercial Club banquet staged last Thursday, aside from being one of the most enjoyable and most successful occasions of its kind ever staged in the village, was also one of the most unique events of its kind ever held in this part of the state.

"The banquet was successful from the standpoint of attendance, over one hundred partaking, successful also because of the general spirit of good cheer and sociability which pervaded, the fine eatables served, and the interesting program.

"But the unique feature was called to attention by Rev. Philip Gordon, toastmaster for the evening, who in his inimitable, humorous way, pointed out that the banquet was being held in the dining room of a Swedish Lutheran Church, with the

pastor of the church asking grace at the beginning and pronounc-
ing the benediction at the close; the band was under the direction
of the pastor of the German Lutheran Church; the Methodist
pastor was on the speaking program; the toastmaster was the
pastor of an Irish Catholic parish; of the three members of the
committee in charge, one was an Englishman, one a Dane, and
one a German; the main speaker of the evening was a Scotchman;
the entertainer of the evening gave Italian and French dialect
readings as part of the program; and to further complete the
mixture, there was one real American present — an Indian —
no one, but the Rev. Gordon."

CHAPTER
XIV
Indian Priest and the Irish

~~~~~~

IN JANUARY, 1926, DEAR FRIENDS OF FATHER GORDON, MAJOR
J. Frank Quilty and his wife of Chicago, Ill., made it possible
for Father Gordon to take a three-week vacation by way of a
lecture trip to Florida. He spoke at Daytona Beach, Mt. Dora,
Leesburn, Clermont, Winter Haven, Bradenton, Lakeland, and
Clearwater. He met many Wisconsin people all over, but found
race prejudice strong, with Jim Crow cars used by law on all the
railroads. Negroes had their own waiting rooms, cars, places in
the busses, etc.

At that time he said, "Give me good old Wisconsin. We have
a variety of climate here. Good roads. Bob LaFollette — and
as a man told me down in Florida, 'Prohibition is better than no
liquor at all.' "

A Florida publication called him "a most fascinating and
lovable member of his race as he pointed out to the Open Forum
audience last Sunday afternoon interesting and pathetic facts about
present day life on reservations."

In writing the History of St. Pat's in the 1940's Father Gordon
recalled the lectures in Florida. He said "I refrain from repeating
the address because many will learn how old the jokes are that
I still use in my talks."

Father Gordon continued to use the old parish house at Long Lake. Charlie Turner said the money was there to build a new one and he asked the priest why he didn't go ahead and build.

"Oh, I won't be here long and I wouldn't want to build a house that maybe the next person wouldn't like."

Charlie was proud to say the parish had the unusual distinction of never being in debt, and he is upset now that some want to build a church for the tourists. The old building that had housed the chapel had been turned into a tavern and hardware store.

Sinon Lynch tells of taking the priest from his house at Long Lake to the church in Centuria.

"One Sunday it was snowing terrific and blowing and we were about halfway out and he said, 'Sinon, if next Sunday is like this, we're not going out.' It was snowing and blowing so much the horses had to pick their way. It was about four miles from the old parsonage to the church."

Sinon recalls that Father Gordon was always on time. "Not before, not after. He was awful punctual."

The Long Lake Cemetery is still there, with names representing many nationalities, but mostly Irish. As Charlie Turner says, "Long Lake was all Irish years ago and almost all related. Centuria was all Swedes; Milltown, all Danes. Between them was the Irish and they kept the Danes and Swedes from fighting." There were others who said it took an Indian to keep the Irish from fighting.

Father Gordon's well-known sense of humor made him compatible with the Irish community. In an article in *Badger Trails,* No. 24, May 9, 1928, entitled "Indian Priest Makes Good in Irish Parish," John H. Lienhard wrote, "When a Chippewa Indian priest was sent four years ago to take charge of the Irish parish of St. Patrick's, embracing almost half of Polk county, some persons were skeptical.

"But not for long. Father Philip Gordon came down from Reserve and proceeded to show them that any one who has played left end for St. Thomas college at St. Paul three years is a good cnough Irishman to run any kind of a parish. Now he ranks with Sheriff Jim Olson at Balsam Lake as one of the two most popular men in the county.

"St. Croix Falls, Luck, Centuria, Balsam Lake, and Milltown are all in Rev. Father Gordon's parish as well as Long Lake where he lives in the parish house with his father as housekeeper. There are five public high schools and 25 district schools in his parish.

"He is scout master of Centuria Troop No. 2, Boy Scouts of America. He is largely interested in the work of the Parent-Teacher associations and addresses their meeting as well as the various high schools in the parish. Every year he gives a big parish picnic with Indian dances and notable speakers.

"The last one was attended by Governor Fred Zimmerman of Wisconsin, Tommy Gibbons of St. Paul, former heavyweight boxing aspirant, and Chad Smith, St. Paul airmail pilot."

Charlie Turner said if Father had anything to say to anybody he often brought it out in his sermon.

"I had a sister," Charlie said, "that rode to the city with him. So he was telling during his sermon, 'I never knew that the ladies of the parish were so religious as they are.' He said, 'You know I took a lady down to the city. She wanted to go to the city and I was going down and she rode along. She sat in the back seat and you know, she didn't know I saw it, but I think she blessed herself twenty times on the way.'

"Oh, he drove fast. He was a wonderful driver. I never heard of him having an accident and he always had a big car, a heavy car, but he could see in the looking glass and she blessed herself twenty times." Fast, at that time, was probably about 35 miles per hour.

Even his father agreed that Father Gordon was a fast driver. He said, "My, how fast my son drives. I do not want to ride with him." But he also said, "My son is a smart Indian." Father Gordon had to drive fast to keep up with his many activities.

Charlie Turner said, "He was a wonderful person. He had a

way of telling you to do things. I never went to a dance during
Lent and we was brought up quite strict. But there was about a
dozen married couples went to dances during the year and being
I knew Father so well, they wanted me to go and ask if it would
be alright to dance on St. Patrick's Day.

"And you know, I got the most beautiful answer that I ever
heard. He says, 'You know I don't see no harm in it but I'm
sure St. Patrick won't thank you.' And we didn't go. Now he
didn't say right out, 'No, you can't go.' Now, you couldn't go
after that."

The priest's aunt, Tressie Lynch, 87, who is living in a
nursing home said Father Gordon had many, many friends. Her
son was the first baby he baptized in Centuria.

Mr. and Mrs. Lawrence Reidner still lived near the church in
1975. Mrs. Reidner remembered when they had a little hotel in
Centuria and Father Gordon would eat dinner there.

"He ate there lots of times. He was always in a hurry. He'd
eat and go. He didn't wait for dessert; if you didn't have the
dessert right there, he'd be gone. He was always busy.

"The first time I met him, I lived in St. Paul and he brought
a basketball team down to St. James Church in our neighborhood.
After a while I got pretty well acquainted with him. He sponsored
a girl's basketball team, too."

The Reidners described Father Gordon as being a big man, a
little on the plump side, but his father, who lived with him for
some years, was a tall, slender man.

Father Gordon liked good food, and Mrs. Reidner recalls that,
back in those days, Catholics had strictly enforced abstinence
from meat on Friday. Those were the days when the "thrashing"
crew moved from farm to farm with a gigantic threshing machine
run by a long belt attached to a powerful, chugging, wheezing
steam engine. Farmers' wives loaded the tables with huge platters
of meat, bowls of mashed potatoes, gravy, vegetables, homemade
pickles, and pies and cakes.

When the farmer knew the threshing crew would be coming

on Friday, he would get permission from the priest to serve meat to the large group of men they would be having for meals. So the priest always knew where the good meals were going to be served. That was where Father Gordon had dinner that Friday. In fact, he had been known to ask one of his farmer friends to try to have the threshers on a Friday.

Father Gordon loved children and he had an impact on them. Russell H. Johnson, now senior vice-president of the First National Bank of St. Paul, tells how Father Gordon made a bow and arrow for him. Mr. Johnson's parents had a store in Centuria. When he was seven or eight years old, around 1925, the priest sat in the back room of the store and whittled out Russell's first bow and arrow from an apple crate. No doubt he made many more for other children.

Even with his busy schedule, the priest found time to sponsor both boy's and girl's basketball teams and other athletics. He was Scout Master, which eventually led to the presentation of the drum and peace pipe to the St. Paul Troop which finally went to President Kennedy.

CHAPTER XV

More Indian Problems

~~~~~~

FATHER GORDON WAS NOT ALONE IN HIS FIGHT FOR THE rights of the Indians. According to an article in the Minneapolis *Journal,* May 23, 1925, "Indians of Wisconsin have been swindled out of millions of dollars in land and timber, investigators of conditions on the Odanah Reservation declare, and a thorough investigation of the charges is now under way.

"Complete restoration of the value of the plundered property is demanded if the evidence reveals irregularities as charged, in a resolution passed by the legislature, which directed the governor and the attorney general to begin legal action against federal and state agencies as may be necessary to accomplish this result.

"Daniel W. Grady, attorney of Portage, has been retained by the state to begin the investigation and he has already started the work.

"Charges that the Indians have been swindled out of money as a result of timber cuttings were first brought to public attention by E. P. Wheeler of Aurora, Ill. Mr. Wheeler's father was a missionary among the Indians on the Bad River Reservation in Ashland County. . . ."

John Collier, U. S. Commissioner of Indian Affairs, said, "The tragic chapter has not ended, and it will not end, save with annihilation, unless states like Wisconsin move promptly, demanding reforms in the federal administration and assuming directly, as states, their own share of responsibility.

"The anomaly of the Indian's situation has now been increased. Congress in June made all Indians citizens of the states. Thus the burden of educating them, of protecting their health, and caring for their indigent and aged, is thrown mandatorily on the states. But the federal guardianship over the Indian's person is maintained intact; and the federal trusteeship over the still enormous Indian estate remains absolute and unregenerate.

"Already tens of thousands of Indians have become, in an inescapable physical sense, charges upon the states. Now they are made legal charges."

Father Gordon called this time "the saddest in the long and losing fight of the Indians for elemental human rights." But there was more to come.

He made another attempt to secure an Indian parish. In a lengthy letter to the Apostolic Delegate in Washington, D. C., he repeated the history of Reserve, told of the success of the mission and of the degeneration of the Indians since he left.

". . . The number of comments by way of letters addressed to the writer from his wide circle of friends both in the ranks of the clergy and from devoted lay people asking for information and sometimes even criticizing his 'desertion' of his Indians is surprising and disquieting and has at length led him to compose this letter. . . .

"The fact that causes me personal grief is that I am an Indian and am deprived of the opportunity to work for my own. Work in the Indian mission field is one of great privation and bitter experience because of the childish prejudices, the ignorance, the illiteracy, the primitive conditions obtaining among Indian people, the lack of financial support, and the general indifference and apathy of all concerned. I know all this and have experienced it. Nevertheless, I feel so affected by the present conditions that I am quite willing to forsake all else in life to render succor to the Indians whose faith is indeed in peril. . . .

"We can say with pride that I have never questioned the judgment of my bishop, have never inquired into his motive of my transfer, have never criticized his action in the matter, even though I have often wondered at his secretive methods, his apparent lack of confidence, and his securing of information from people who are so openly notorious and so opposed to things Catholic.

"At any rate, I do not sincerely believe that all is right in this matter and it may develop that I am a criminal without knowing it, or it may be shown that the good judgment of the Bishop of Superior is indeed superior to the well-known wishes of the present Pontiff, Pius XI, 'a native clergy for the native people in every land.' "

As to the consequences of the letter, Father Gordon said, "We know of none attributed directly to this appeal for action and justice."

Although the Indian priest had mellowed with the passing years and his attitude was not as militant as in the early part of his priesthood, he could not be reconciled to many of the rules and regulations imposed by the government. One that irked him particularly in 1926 was the attempted restriction of Indian dances.

The Indians defied the order and Father Gordon continued to have the Indian dances at his annual parish picnics. He always brought his Indian friends from the reservation — Johnnie Frog, George James, Willie Debrot, and others.

When plans were made for the third annual picnic, Senator Irvine L. Lenroot was to be the principal guest and speaker. He was familiarly known to the Chippewas as A-Ka-Bi-Ji-Bik, The Root. Congressman Frear and Ray J. Nye, of Superior, Federal Prohibition Director, also accepted Father Gordon's invitation.

He arranged a meeting for the Indians so they could present a petition to Senator Lenroot against the attempted suppression of the Indian recreative dances, principally the war dance. He also spoke of this suppression at an anniversary celebration which is quoted in the St. Paul *Daily News* on August 22, 1926:

" 'The American Indian will not abandon the tribal dances, at least not without stubborn resistance.'

"This is the opinion of Rev. Philip Gordon, himself a full-blooded Chippewa, who will conduct the 11 a.m. service today, final day of the 19th anniversary celebration in Hazel Park of the Church of the Blessed Sacrament at White Bear.

"Featuring the afternoon program will be several Indian dances by about 50 braves and 80 squaws from the Courtes Oreilles reservation in Sawyer county, Wis.

"Included among these dances will be some which certain officials of the federal Indian bureau are seeking to prohibit on the ground that their continuance only retards the complete civilization of the original Americans.

" 'There is really no good ground for such a contention,' declared Father Gordon Saturday night, 'not any more than dancing the waltz or the Charleston among their white brethren.

" 'The different tribal dances constitute about all there is left to the present day Indians to connect them with their savage ancestors who roamed the prairies and woods of America before this continent was discovered. The dances are a tradition with them, and are consequently dear to the heart of every Indian.

" 'Some of the dances are ceremonial in nature, others are indulged in merely for recreation and entertainment, just as white folks do. The federal government officials are in for a difficult job if any serious attempt is made to deprive the Indians of this traditional custom. . . .' "

Father Gordon believed dancing, when properly conducted, was healthy recreation. He objected to "late hours, decollete, escorting, moonshine, etc.," and said some dancing was revolting to every feeling of decency and propriety, but he believed the Indian dances were no more objectionable than dancing the waltz or the Charleston.

The question of Indian affairs arose again when President Calvin Coolidge chose the Brule River as the spot for his 1928 summer vacation. Numerous requests came to Father Gordon to use his influence to have the president meet with delegations of Indians. Some wished the delegation to be dressed in full Indian regalia. Others thought only educated Indians, professional and university men, or men or women who had established themselves in community life should compose such a delegation.

The president received the group dressed in Indian costumes, but no provision was made to meet with the educated Indians.

There was considerable correspondence covering the matter and Father Gordon was allowed an interview with Everett Sanders, Secretary to the President. He was accompanied to the executive offices in Superior by Father James Fagan of that city, but it seems the secretary did not want the President to bother himself with Indian affairs while on vacation and the Indian priest did not get an audience with the President.

Conditions were the same over the entire United States. The Anaconda (Mont.) *Standard* carried an article about the same time, June 22, 1928, stating in part·

"The fact that the Republican party's candidate for vice president has Indian blood in his veins may help to draw public attention to the present pitiable conditions of many, if not of most, of the 350,000 Indians now in the United States. The recent report made by the Institute for Government Research and given out by the Department of the Interior, under which it functions, revealed some shocking facts. Tuberculosis, trachoma, and other diseases, particularly those of infancy, are prevalent among the Indians, the report states. Their death rate is high and living conditions poor. They are badly housed and do not have enough proper food. They are poverty stricken and have not become adjusted to the economic and social life which surrounds them. The Indians do not have proper medical attention. Hospitals are too few and are not well equipped or conducted. The staff of the Indian Bureau is inadequate and underpaid and, in many instances, improperly trained. Schools are insufficient and poorly administered. The Senate Committee on Indian Affairs has taken cognizance of the report and will conduct an inquiry during the summer with the view of making specific recommendations to the end that Congress may act intelligently and justly . . ."

The great problem of getting back the lost lands of the Indians was not touched upon. Many Indians thought the same predatory interests — lumbering principally — were the chief influence in preventing disclosure. Investigation after investigation failed to bring results.

In 1929 a bill was introduced in the Wisconsin Legislature which would have provided that the Attorney General of Wisconsin would be empowered to appoint special attorneys to prosecute the claims of the Indians in the United States Court of Claims. It was passed by an almost unanimous vote only to be vetoed by Governor Kohler.

The Congressman wrote Father Gordon urging him to get in touch with every Indian friend and acquaintance throughout Wisconsin and have them write to their Assemblymen and Senators urging them to pass this bill over the governor's veto.

During this same time a controversy, lasting two years, was going on with reference to the action of representatives of the Wisconsin State Conservation Commission on entering the U. S. Indian warehouse and seizing certain hides including some belonging to George James. Of course, an investigation was made.

CHAPTER
XVI
Problems on the Farm

As with every priest, Father Gordon had a long list of regular priestly duties that were a regular routine — "Breviary, Mass, Rosary, Spiritual Reading, Exams, and the constant interest in souls, sick-calls, deaths, births, marriages, debts, collections, sermons, confessions, communions, catechism, vocational schools, retreats, confirmations, devotions, virtue, sin. . . ."

Still he always found time to help where he was needed. When Father O'Hara (later Bishop of Kansas City) urged the attention of the Catholic Church to the rural question, the National Catholic Rural Life Conference was formed as part of the Social Action Department of the National Catholic Welfare Conference. Father Gordon soon became involved and attended the third annual meeting in St. Paul, October 12-17, 1925.

The Conference regarded the betterment of rural conditions as the starting point in the regeneration of society. Its objectives were the improvement of the spiritual, religious, social, cultural, and economic status of the rural group.

They stated: "Reconquest of the soil, which has been depleted through improper use and exploitation, is a fundamental consideration, for human erosion is closely related to soil erosion. Reconquest of ownership is another fundamental consideration, inasmuch as ownership is essential for independent, successful, and self-satisfying farm life. The multiplying of family-sized, owner-operated farms is an important safeguard against the exploitation of our greatest natural resource, namely, the land. . . ."

When he was unable to attend a conference because of distance, Father Gordon kept in touch with everything that was going on and read everything about the conferences. He was an avid reader and had an uncanny ability to absorb what he read.

Many important subjects were discussed at the conferences — A Review of the Problem of Land Tenancy; Population Prospects in the South; Religion and Rural Welfare; Catholic Rural Social Planning; Youth Problems in Rural Communities; A Christian Interpretation of the More Abundant Life; — and many others.

When the national administrator of the Farm Security Administration (FSA), C. B. Baldwin, along with other officials, came to a meeting in St. Cloud, Minn., Father Gordon asked, "Why should one of the largest government agencies . . . send three of the highest ranking men to an abbey in central Minnesota where fewer than one hundred priests and laymen were at school?"

Mr. Baldwin answered, "We are trying to give the low income farmers an outlet for self-expression that they've been lacking. We want to give them dignity, a place in the community. . . . Our experience with disadvantaged citizens has indicated that they are worthy of all the help we can give them. Our legislative fight will be a never-ending fight. We have had a lot of support. I want to pay special tribute to Father Ligutti and to Father O'Grady who have helped us to protect this program that we tried to build so carefully. If it had not been for the assistance that we got from the Farmers Union, from the Catholic Rural Life Conference, and from some labor quarters, I doubt if this work which we are doing could have been saved."

"Mr. Baldwin's tribute also explains why the Church is interested in the FSA. This agency above all on the New Deal program has dealt positively with the common man," Father

Gordon said. "Its object is to protect and promote the family type farm, and in all its divisions it works through the family. It has not simply doled out relief, but in a brilliant, far-sighted program it provides financial and expert guidance over a long period of time so that families can rehabilitate themselves. . . ."

Father Gordon said the meeting brought out the persistence of the same old farm problems so wisely described by Bishop Vincent J. Ryan, of Bismarck, North Dakota:

"A blight has fallen upon the land which tends to destroy everything that is beautiful to behold. At its worst this blight is symbolized by the dispossessed farmer who is now a tenant, dilapidated farm buildings, the hovels of the farm laborers and sharecroppers, the mighty hoards of dispossessed farm families moving across the western sections of the nation in search of work, and the rural proletariat gathering in the towns and cities of the nation."

He said President Roosevelt spoke of this same picture when he proclaimed that one-third of our people are underfed, poorly clothed, and without proper housing.

He also quoted Pope Pius XI who had said a long time ago, "Economic life has become hard, cruel, and relentless in a ghastly manner. Not alone is wealth accumulated, but immense power and despotic economic domination is concentrated in the hands of the few."

Father Gordon added his comment, "I trust this description of present day history will bear fruit in making one or the other farmer at least devote some THOUGHT to his situation and then join to cooperate in the execution of the plans suggested by his friends and in this case, by his friend the Catholic Church."

Previous to this time it had been true that the farmer was an isolationist by necessity. His neighbors were far away and there was little contact because of poor roads, no phones, and not much group action.

Father Gordon said, "This bred a sort of exclusive regard for one's own personal interest — nothing else than selfishness. So here we have perhaps another reason for the farmer's lack of appreciation of cooperation. . . ."

He worked zealously to promote the Farmers' Union and preached adult education. He was in demand as a speaker at meetings, picnics, school commencements, etc., where he urged farmers to join the union and also took the occasion to speak of the rising juvenile delinquency. In June 1942, he prepared broadcasts in German and Italian on Station KSTP, St. Paul, for the Office of Strategic Services.

He had his own philosophy in regard to the state of the world, in disagreement with the economists, socialists, and capitalists. Their theories, he said, were "examples of modern man looking outside of himself to explain the chaos that is gradually forming in the world. If only he would look inside himself and examine his conscience, he would find the real answer — it is the almost universal *rejection by mankind of Christian principles.*"

An article in the *Christian Farmer,* December, 1940 stated, "The same jungle law we also find prevailing in agriculture, which makes agriculture as bad off as the rest of the modern economic system. Despite policies and programs, good intentions and organizations, the lot of the farmer of today is no better than it was years ago; if anything it is worse."

"What is almost a surprise to me," Father Gordon said, "is that most of the sugestions and plans of action offered by the National C.R.L.C. (Catholic Rural Life Conference) were offered to us fifteen years ago. To indicate what progress has been made or I should say, lack of progress, I would only have to list the number of farm foreclosures that has taken place in my little flock. . . ."

He also berated the clergy for lack of interest — "I am still waiting to see my brothers of the cloth (this is an expression used to designate clergymen) become indignant over the woes of the farmer. Some are interested in foreign missions and take collections for the heathen in far-off China. Others are interested in Madagascar or Manchuria, but Polk County counts many

farmers living in absolute insecurity, and few seem interested. . . .
Preachers preach 'Love Thy Neighbor' and promptly forget the
neighbor, apparently. . . ."

When 1,000 indignant farmers from four counties met in
Sparta to begin a determined fight against the Federal Security
Administration's ruling which permitted the use of synthetic
vitamins in manufacturing oleomargarine, he asked, "Where in
Polk County is an organization to join in this battle?"

The St. Cloud *Daily Times*, Thursday, August 8, 1942, quoted
Father Gordon, after the meeting there, "I live in Polk County,
and it is the most cooperative-minded county in the whole United
States. My parish includes five country villages, and in one,
Milltown, cooperative promoters from all over the United States
and Canada come to hold their annual meeting. . . .

"Eighty percent of the people in the county are of Danish,
Swedish, and Norwegian extraction. Hence they brought their
cooperative ideas and plans from Europe. We have the oldest
cooperative newspaper establishment. The county is filled with
cooperative creameries, cheese factories, and milk drying estab-
lishments. . . ." But the farmers were reluctant to unite.

After World War II began, the economy vastly changed, "but
certainly not for the better," Father Gordon said, "particularly
when we look ahead say five years from now."

CHAPTER
XVII
More KKK and Other Problems

THERE WERE MANY WHO HAD CONSIDERED THE PRIEST'S appointment to the little town in northwestern Wisconsin a place of isolation, but it did not prove so to Father Gordon. He was forty-eight when he came to Long Lake, but he began his most active period of public life. He was in demand as a speaker; he maintained his interest in Indian affairs; he took an active part in farmer's organizations and especially the Farmers' Union; he was interested in politics in which he was a liberal in the La Follette tradition. He supported Franklin Roosevelt and was a firm backer of Henry A. Wallace as Secretary of Agriculture. The Wallace and Gordon families became good friends.

The Indian priest loved to travel and did so at every opportunity. He often made trips to the reservations and was asked to speak at many different events. On several occasions he attended the Eucharistic Congress in Europe and the United States.

One of the first ones in which he was involved was in Chicago in 1926. He made the trip by automobile, taking along a number of Indians. They were guests there at the Slovenian meeting. This was the nationality of the first missionary to bring the gospel to the Chippewa Indians and to do effective work among them,

Bishop Baraga. Father Gordon spoke in German at the Innsbruck Alumni meeting at the Congress.

A newspaper account dramatically described the Congress ". . . a historical painting such as one comes upon in galleries of the old world was now touched to life and to actuality.

"Banners softly swaying; high aloft enormous golden garlands of grape leaves and bunches of grapes; sheaves of the goodly wheat; triple crowns of gold interlaced with silver fabric; Knights of the Holy See in ceremonial cloaks partly revealing coat sleeves heavily embroidered with gold and silver; colossal replicas of the papal arms. . . . And here — ah, marvelous continuity and comprehensiveness of the Church's story — an American Indian wearing the feathered ceremonial headdress of the Chippewas. That Indian is a priest now and known and loved among his people and your people at Centuria, Wisconsin, as Father Philip Gordon. . . ."

It was during this week, June 20-24, 1926, that the KKK activities caused some commotion in the neighboring county of St. Croix. A Mr. Alfred Brown was engaged in a series of violent anti-Catholic talks in that county.

Father Gordon wrote, "I do not know if he disgraced any Protestant ministry by calling himself a Reverend or attached himself to any particular denomination."

On June 11, Mr. Fred L. Rothgeber, editor of the newspaper in Clear Lake, Polk County, wrote the following letter to Father Gordon:

"Dear Sir: I would be pleased to have the pleasure of arranging a debate between yourself and Mr. Alfred Brown in the immediate future on the following subject: Resolved that the Roman hierarchy is an un-American organization.

"Please advise me of your acceptance or objection of the opportunity to debate Mr. Brown on the above subject at your earliest convenience.

"Respectfully,
"Fred L. Rothgeber, P.O. Box 56."

Father Gordon replied and suggested a date after the Eucharistic Congress which he planned to attend. After an exchange of letters, on June 21, Mr. Rothgeber wrote, "It is my opinion and I believe you will agree with me that it is advisable to abandon further effort to complete arrangements for a debate on the subject mentioned in previous letters, after the recent happenings at Northline, because it may incite, or create, religious hatred."

The "recent happenings" referred to was the burning of Mr. Brown's tent by a group from Hudson. Some of the disturbers of the peace were subsequently arrested and court proceedings initiated. Father Rice, then at Hudson, was instrumental in abolishing the KKK from the area.

When Father Gordon traveled to Dublin, Ireland, in 1932 to attend the Eucharistic Congress there, he was a member of a party of about a hundred pilgrims from St. Paul.

The St. Paul *Pioneer Press* noted, "A full-blooded Indian priest of the Chippewa tribe who appeared in the regalia of his people in a procession at the Congress, is the 'star' of a film made there.

"Rev. Philip Gordon of Centuria, Wis. . . . steals the show from the conventionally dressed cardinals and the pope's legate who marched in the procession. More than a million persons from all parts of the world attended the Congress. . . ."

The film, which also included scenes taken in Germany was filmed by Rev. Leon M. Linden of Aurora, Ill. and was exhibited for the benefit of unemployed workers of St. Paul.

While in Ireland, Father Gordon met prominent Irishmen and spent a day as the guest of Eaman de Valera, prime minister, who had visited at the mission at Reserve.

The following year the St. Paul *Dispatch* published an article which stated: "The only American Indian Catholic priest in the world, Rev. Philip Gordon of Centuria, Wis., will help lead a Holy Year mission pilgrimage from St. Paul to Rome in July.

"He will assist Rev. James A. Troy, 244 Dayton Avenue, director of the Society for the Propagation of the Faith, in guiding Northwest pilgrims along European travel trails far different from the trails trod by his ancestors through Chippewa forests. . . ."

The tour included visits to many historic places as well as a four-day stay in Rome where they had an audience with Pope Pius XI, the Pope of the Missions.

Wherever he went, Father Gordon always rated write-ups in the newspapers. Of these he said, "The so-called 'write-ups' that always were bound to appear in the local newspapers 'on a visit of an Indian priest' and which had become sort of stereotyped must by now become a nuisance to the patient readers of these historical notes."

But they always appeared. In 1929, on an eastern trip, he was quoted in the Trenton *Times,* "The poverty existing among the Indian tribes in the United States is simply appalling. He quoted the survey recently completed by the Bureau of Government research to prove that widespread poverty, which verges upon actual starvation, can be found on many Indian Reservations. . . ."

Another sidelight of that trip which amused him was what he called a literary curiosity, a write-up in a Hungarian newspaper, published in Trenton, called "Uj Vilag." There were about twenty-five paragraphs, which he said amounted to this, "The fellow is alright."

Like all clergy, Father Gordon constantly encountered problems, but his sense of humor helped to carry him through many of his trials. In his History of St. Pat's he mentioned "two remarkable letters, but not unusual. It would be 'rich reading' if these letters could be submitted, but they deal more or less with private, almost confidential matters. I mention them, however, because it is indicative of the fact that the priest is sometimes bombarded with propaganda and subjected to quite a bit of pressure if someone's feelings have been hurt by enforcement of Church rules and regulations.

"One of the above letters was in response to a statement sent out by the then secretary of the parish, Wm. Cosgrove. He was dunning delinquent members. One such member (it happened to be a woman) wrote a long and involved statement full of dates and figures and additions and subtractions with considerable sarcasm and even bitterness. . . . The letter was so long and hefty that it took 4¢ postage. The woman subsequently died and I often prayed that I hoped St. Peter was a good mathematician to figure out if the family in question had all the pew rent paid up.

"The second letter was an involved marriage case. It was written by an irate Irishman who talked plenty tough. However, the eventual outcome of this matter was that the state law in Minnesota intervened and the marriage was dissolved when one of the parties landed in the state 'pen,' and thereafter the pastor could sleep without wild dreams.

"It might be interesting to note that an average of about three or four goofy letters reach a priest each month from all sorts of odd characters. While I love to receive friendly and good letters, I also get a kick out of reading some of the effusions of people who may disagree with me. At the worst, it can be said that most correspondence is meant to be sincere."

Some members of Father Gordon's parish also felt there was discrimination against the Catholics in the public schools. Now and then it was brought to his attention that applicants for a position were asked what religious denomination he or she belonged to and the applicant failed to land the job.

"I had this particular complaint with reference to the St. Croix Falls College and High School. We never entered into the allegations against this school but there was this bald fact that often caused me to wonder. In all the eighteen years of pastorate of this writer in Polk County, there has been but one Catholic, to our knowledge, teaching in St. Croix Falls, although all neighboring schools — Luck, Milltown, Balsam Lake, Centuria, Frederic, Amery, Osceola, Webster, Cumberland, etc. — are seldom without teachers and instructors and even principals who practice the Catholic religion. Not that the school boards are respectively Catholic or anti-Catholic.

"Incidentally, it might be put down as a most remarkable

coincidence that this pastor (of St. Patrick's Church, which includes St. Croix Falls) has not once been invited to offer an invocation, give a benediction, recite a baccalaureate, offer a commencement address (our charges have only been for gas and oil instead of the $25.00 given to out-of-town speakers) in that school in his parish.

"This fact has never been interpreted as meant to be a deliberate slight but matched with other happenings might give rise to suspicion in sensitive minds, particularly to the Catholics patronizing a particular school, inasmuch as the writer has often been called upon to help with his poor talents in Public School exercises of various kinds in the high schools located in the parish, as well as elsewhere. . . ."

In answer to a letter, State Superintendent John Callahan explained that "the question of religious denomination is never considered in applications for positions as teachers in the public schools. . . .

"The department is, however, well aware that in some sections of the state applications for positions are rejected on account of religious preference, and the selection is probably decided to a greater or less extent by community disposition. . . ."

Often unhappy events caused the priest sorrow, but they never made him submissive. As a "sample of the 'doings' in some parts of the Land of the Free and the Home of the Brave," he entered the following in his reminiscences:

"From the *Polk County Ledger*, Balsam Lake, Wis. —

"OPEN FORUM

" (Opinions expressed and statements made are those of the writers and do not necessarily reflect the views of the paper.)

"NO INDIANS WANTED

"We, the people of Georgetown and Johnstown, living near Big Round Lake, are very bitter against having an Indian Reserve put in up here. We have no canned heat factory up here to keep them warm.

"A much better place is at Balsam Lake, if they must be kept in the county. There they could have the benefit of good schools, county nurse, everlasting job for relief department which is so well established in the county garage, and by putting in floor on the beams which support the roof in the county garage, they could house the whole tribe and keep them warm and save canned heat. We have too many Indians here now such as they are. It will only mean a long war to the bitter end. Not only with Indians, but with the people who are trying to put them on us.

"We have a wonderful place for a game refuge and intend to establish one here. Already we have plenty of deer, a start of beavers, muskrats, ring necks, and grouse. We are about the center of a large deer territory. We have a fish reserve in Big Round Lake and everybody respects it, and thinks it is a good thing. — A Subscriber."

The Game preserve was established near Big Round Lake.

"Editor's Note: We can well leave it to the prowess of Father Gordon to take care of 'Subscriber' when the time comes to talk about the matter."

CHAPTER
XVIII
An Unforgettable Journey

MANY PEOPLE FROM ST. PAUL, MINN., WHO VACATIONED AT summer resorts or their private cabins at the lakes in his parish, became acquainted with Father Gordon. Among them was the family of Louis Villaume, descendant of one of St. Paul's pioneer families.

Their names are still on the register at The Shores Resort (formerly Calderwood Springs) on Bone Lake. On June 23, 1925, the Villaume family is listed, with Father Gordon directly underneath. The next year the name of Thomas Gibbons appears. He was world heavyweight contender who fought and was defeated by Jack Dempsey. He was there to buy land that later became St. Luke's Camp for St. Luke's Church in St. Paul. He became a good friend of Father Gordon.

Paul Villaume vividly remembers the priest. He says, "My first memory of Father Philip Gordon was in 1925 at Calderwood Springs Resort at Bone Lake in Polk County. Father Gordon came on Sunday morning to conduct Mass on the front porch of Mr. Calder's summer cabin. At that time he had already begun to form a Boy Scout troop and my brother Louis was one of the original members."

All the Villaume children were confirmed in St. Patrick's Church; and Paul says, "It was my great honor to have William Gordon, the priest's father, as my sponsor."

After his confirmation, Paul Villaume made the first of his many trips with Father Gordon to the Court Oreilles Reservation, near Hayward, Wis. The Indians gave him the name Ka-Wah-Din, which in Chippewa means "North Wind."

"There was an informal ceremony," he says. " 'The Chief' and a number of Indians beat the drums. I was thirteen years old, and I'm sure I was more impressed than they were about the occasion." The priest was affectionately known by the family as "the Chief."

Later, Paul's ego was somewhat deflated when his father told him his Indian name actually meant "Hot Air."

From 1929 to 1936 the Villaume family spent the summers at Perry Mound on Balsam Lake. They became close friends of the Indian priest and Paul was often in his company. In fact, he had a room at the rectory for many years. At that time, William Gordon was the housekeeper. He was 75 when his priest son was assigned to St. Patrick's.

The Chief later reminisced, "My father was a great cook. Good, plain, substantial cooking — the sort he used to do when he was a cook in the lumber camps. I don't believe there was anyone who could bake a pot of beans lumber camp style like he could. That was his speciality. I think of him still, out there in the kitchen, frequently stirring the pot of beans in the oven so that they would be just right. And when it came to cooking wild game he was the equal of the best."

There was always wild rice on the table, an Indian staple from which Father Gordon was never far removed. He made many visits to the reservations and kept in touch with his Indian friends and their customs. He also frequently visited his mother, who had gone back to the reservation.

He liked to hunt and fish and would always be seen wearing a hat, but still he suffered a sunburned nose. He often wore a hat on other occasions, too, and especially liked a straw hat known as a "sailor."

Even with all his activities the priest had not forgotten his old college days. On May 21, 1931, he was among 175 former St. Thomas College athletes who attended the first annual homecoming of the Monogram Club. Athletic teams from as far back as 1896 were represented in the group. They decided to make the reunion an annual affair. Before the 1933 reunion, when Father Gordon was to be given an honorary Doctor's degree, he wrote to Rev. W. F. Cunningham, C.S.C., Dean of Studies at St. Thomas, "It is indeed a great privilege for me to be associated with the activities of the Holy Cross Fathers in their educational work at my old College. Of course, it is a matter of extreme pleasure to me to think that I have been designated by the Administration for the honor of an honorary degree. I feel myself an unworthy candidate for such a distinction.

"In reply to your suggestion as to ordering a Doctor's gown, I should like to have one at the minimum price. The specifications you asked for are as follows:

"Weight 220; Height 5′ 11½″; Size of Hat 6⅞, or 7. As I expect to participate in the Monogram Banquet, I shall endeavor to have a check for the gown to give you then."

It was apparent from the letter he no longer had the trim athletic figure of his college days. One of his classmates had been urging him to write a book on the religious opportunities among the Indians or any related subject. He chided the priest, "Next to my solicitude to have you regain your previous athletic slim figure, this other ambition of mine to have you write, ranks second."

Paul Villaume says, "The Chief was a big man. In the 1930's and early '40's he weighed in excess of 200 pounds. He always drove a big car. The first car I recall he had was an Auburn touring car. Then he had a Chevrolet coupé, the first one they made in 1926, I believe.

"But the car he loved most, I think because of the color, was a Lincoln Zephyr coupé which was fire-engine red. One of the local chiefs wanted him to paint it another color because in those days they didn't have red automobiles. Father Gordon claimed that since red was an Indian color he thought he would keep his car red. When anybody saw a red car it was either Chief Gordon or the fire chief."

The priest's reputation as a driver was not the best; but he never had an accident, which was probably only accountable to the sparse traffic at the time. Paul told his father, after a trip with Father Gordon, "I'm going to become a priest because I could drive on either side of the road and get there."

Father Gordon had serious surgery around this time and was given but a few months to live. "Malignant carcinoma" was the diagnosis. He gives Dr. William Carroll credit for helping to save his life. After he had sufficiently recovered, he suggested a trip to his young friend.

In 1934, Father Gordon and Paul Villaume sailed on a three month's trip to the Mediterranean. Everyone realized what a splendid opportunity this would be for a young man of eighteen. Among the letters he received was one from his mother which shows the high regard the family had for the priest. She sent the letter so he would receive it as his ship sailed.

"My dear boy: When you receive this letter, you will have started on one of life's great journeys. You are a very lucky boy to have a friend like Father Gordon. It means much in life to know such a person. We are all happy to number him among our friends and it is our wish that you do all in your power to make Father Gordon's trip a perfect one.

"I am so glad your father will be able to wave to you as your boat departs as it does so warm the heart . . .

"Make the most of each day and have rest and be happy. We shall all miss you. Love from all, Mother."

A friend in the mayor's office, Catherine Aynsley, wrote at length of the "marvelous opportunity." She said, ". . . I know you are going to see many sights and learn many things to enrich your mind that you will carry through your entire life. You are most fortunate in having so fine a traveling companion as Father Gordon and I will be glad if you will give my best wishes to him.

"You are traveling a long way from the home territory and I know there will be days when you will wish you were under your home roof, but try and get as much as you can out of each day, and your friends, as well as your family, will be most glad to welcome you back to our fair city when your journey is ended.

"I hope the 'bombardments' now going on in Austria and France are going to be over and settled soon so as not to interfere with your plans.

"We are still enjoying the same mild sunshiny sort of weather and it is beginning to look like we aren't going to have any winter, but I think a good old fashioned Minnesota snowstorm would be most welcome.

"Georgie and your friend, Joe Kilroy, are still running the P.S.P.A. with a little assistance from Mr. Roosevelt.

"My every best wish is for you and I just hope this wonderful opportunity that has come to you will be followed by others and bring to you much happiness throughout your life."

Paul said, "If we couldn't get in somewhere, we used the letter from the mayor's office. It looked official."

There were two items which Paul carried all over during their trip. One was his mouth organ and the other was the priest's Indian headdress, which he transported in a wooden box. Father Gordon wore it on any and all occasions.

Paul recalls, "He wore it to a dinner which was given in honor of the Egyptian Ambassador to the United States and the ambassador delighted in it. Another time that stands out in my memory was on Easter Sunday, 1934, the day after Father Gordon's birthday. We visited St. Peter's Cathedral in Rome. I suggested he put on his headdress and 10,000 people followed him out onto St. Peter's Square. It was the first time they had ever seen an American Indian headdress other than in American movies."

Although Paul had not learned the prayers or even attended a

Catholic school, he served Mass for the Chief during the three months of their trip.

One of the memories which Paul says is indelibly printed in his mind was when Father Gordon was given special permission to say Mass in the Church of the Holy Sepulcher, built on the site of the crucifixion and burial of Christ.

It was an unforgettable journey for two pals with thirty years difference in their ages. They sailed from New York and shared a stateroom on a North German Lloyd liner, the *Columbus,* which was the largest ship until the *Bremen* and the *Europa* were built.

Paul recalls, "The fare at the time was $346 round trip. The ship was our hotel. We visited Madeira, Casablanca, Gibraltar, went back to Algiers, Tunis, to the French Riviera, Nice, Monte Carlo, Tripoli, the Island of Malta, Sicily, Naples, over to St. Louis where King Louis of France, died. Then we went all the way to the end of the Mediterranean to Lebanon. Then to Palestine where they were building the city of Tel Aviv and from Jerusalem to Cairo, came back and caught the ship at Haifa, to Alexandria, then to Constantinople, through the Dardanelles and the Black Sea. We came to Athens and through Jugo-Slavia, Albania, Venice, Naples, Rome, Florence, Milan, Switzerland, Paris, Lisieux, and sailed from Le Havre."

They met many interesting people wherever they went and had numerous adventures, some rather exciting. One of these is described by Howard Kahn, who wrote under the name of Paul Light in the *Pioneer Press.* He was a good friend of Paul Villaume and often mentioned Father Gordon in his column.

In his column of August 29, 1946, he wrote: "Father Gordon and Paul Villaume (the latter accompanied by his constant companion, a mouth organ) . . . visited Mediterranean countries a few years ago. The priest says he almost lost Paul at Casablanca. The latter decided, as long as he was in the Moroccan metropolis, he should call on the Moroccan sultan. So he went to the palace and rang a bell in the grilled doorway.

"A turbaned, bloomered servant responded. Paul showed him

a letter from Bill Mahoney, then mayor of St. Paul. The letter bore a gold seal of St. Paul and a red, white, and blue ribbon. Paul thinks the servant thought he was a high French official because of the ribbon. The servant admitted him. . . .

"There was a long delay during which Paul felt many eyes peering at him through peep-holes.

"Finally he heard a drum beating. Then he saw a huge Moroccan approaching. One glance told him it wasn't the sultan. The man was in the uniform of the sultan's guard. He was swinging what was probably the largest knife in the world.

"Paul departed immediately for elsewhere. He decided the only person in Casablanca he wanted to see was Father Gordon.

"The latter was surprised when Paul returned to their hotel with his head still attached to his body. . . ."

When he was about to return home, Paul's mother wrote, "How I should love to be there to greet you upon your arrival in your own country which after all is the finest in the world."

The year of the Mediterranean tour was also eventful for Father Gordon's brother who made headlines for a trip he made. James Montreal Gordon, a World War I veteran, known in American Legion circles as "Mike," built a birchbark canoe and learned first-hand the arduous journey his ancestors had made from Lake Superior on the Brule and St. Croix Rivers.

He found the route had not changed too much since his voyageur ancestors arrived in northern Wisconsin. Even today, paddling against the current up the wild Brule, portaging around falls, over the continental divide, down the St. Croix, drifting at times, but backstroking much of the time against the swift current, was strenuous.

He then traveled the entire length of the mighty Mississippi and continued by way of the Inland Waterway to Miami, Fla., to attend a convention of the American Legion. An article in the *Badger Legionnaire*, November 10, 1934, describes some of his experiences on the trip:

". . . Mike, as we call him — and by which name the Miami

crowd will remember him to their dying days — started on his "See Wisconsin First" missionary career when he decided to attend the Miami Convention, and to transport himself there by the means employed by his forefathers; namely, the birchbark canoe. He went up the Brule, portaged to the St. Croix and thus to the Mississippi. He paddled down to New Orleans and by canal into the Gulf to the west coast of Florida, then by canal to the east coast and down to Miami. He spent 83 days paddling 2,939 miles.

"On his way down Mike had 22 speaking engagements before chambers of commerce, high school and college classes, stressing in each the beauties of the good old Badger state which gave him birth, and explaining the ideals of The American Legion of which he is a proud and faithful member."

Orrin McGrath, who was eighty-four in 1975, lived in northern Wisconsin and knew the Gordons. He says, "Jim was a smart fellow. He started out with a big supply of post cards, pictures of himself and his canoe. He sold these and then the various Legion Posts took care of him along the way. He was a congenial cuss. Before he left Miami, he auctioned his canoe and if I remember correctly, he got somewhere between $350 and $400 for that canoe. He was the last canoe builder that I knew."

After their return from the Mediterranean countries, Paul traveled many places with the Chief — to the reservations, to the North Shore of Lake Superior, to Sault Ste. Marie for ceremonies honoring St. Isaac Jogues, the great Jesuit missionary martyr. In 1941, Paul was chairman of a trip of St. Paul civic leaders to Prairie du Chien, Wis., for the 100th anniversary of the first Mass to be said in St. Paul by Father Lucien Galtier who is buried in front of the church and Father Gordon gave the blessing over his grave.

The Indian priest always attended the Bastille Day celebration in St. Paul, an event originated by Paul. He was interested in all the ethnic celebrations. He was proud of being an Indian and so he understood why the Germans were drinking beer and singing and why the Irish had a big parade. He always liked to celebrate with his friends.

In a letter he wrote, "I was much interested in that Bastille Day idea. Good idea, Paul. More than one have asked me why we couldn't have another such blowout. You go ahead and arrange it and I will be there. Could get Father Frank Burns there to make another speech in French and many other things could happen. By all means, get things going for such a gathering. Incidentally, it would please your Dad. Of course, there is supposed to be a ban on non-essential driving but a meeting like that is a help to the war-effort. . . ."

After the eighth annual celebration, the *Pioneer Press* published a photo of some of the participants — Father Gordon; Henri Melancon, New Canada, Paul Villaume, chairman of the celebration; and Dr. Thomas Gehan — with the caption, "Bon Conversation, B'Gorra — You could hardly see the Frenchmen for the Irish. . . . Residents of French descent followed their traditional policy of inviting friends of various nationalities to help mark the 159th anniversary of the storming of the ancient Paris prison during the French revolution. Friends conversed amid mixed choruses of 'La Madelon' and 'My Wild Irish Rose.' "

Paul Light continued to write an occasional item about Father Gordon. In one he mentioned a rain drum Dan Wallace had in his collection of Indian artifacts.

"It once belonged to Two Moons, one of the four Indian chiefs who participated in the Custer massacre. 'It always rains the day after it is played,' Dan insists. 'Father Gordon is very covetous of it. He even offered to take it to Rome and have it blessed by the Pope. But I'm afraid if I let him have it he won't bring it back.'

"The drum has only failed Dan once . . . when he let Father Gordon play it as an accompaniment to some Chippewa songs. It didn't rain, but on the following morning a 3-day blizzard that blocked all roads developed.

" 'Thus,' says Dan, 'you will see the potency of two such medicine men as myself and Father Gordon.' "

Another time the column read, "If you want to order cranberry pie in the Chippewa Indian tongue you ask (approximately) for maski-min-bash ki-min-a-si-gun-wi-we-ga-si-gun-pa-kwe-ji-gun.

"It's about the longest word in the Chippewa language. I use the word 'approximately' because Father Philip Gordon wrote it down for me and I had some difficulty reading his writing. . . . The 45-letter word translates something like this: 'Swamp-berry-cooked-till-it-bursts-wrapping flour-dough-sliced.' "

The priest had a ready wit and a zest for life, but his main interest was always helping those in need — first of all the Indians, but also the Blacks, and the farmers.

CHAPTER
XIX
World War II

THE CHIEF AND PAUL HAD MUTUAL DISAPPOINTMENTS IN their attempts to serve their country in time of war. Father Gordon regretted that he had not been called as chaplain in World War I when he had offered his services. In World War II he was too old and Paul was rejected because of ulcers.

The Chief was proud of the fact that 20,000 of the 320,000 Indians in the United States served in the armed forces and that one of the soldiers who raised the flag at Iwo Jima was an Indian.

They both did what they could to help the war effort at home. Paul had been on the personal staff of Governor Stassen before the war and worked with the Red Cross during the war.

Father Gordon did his bit when German prisoners of war were brought to a camp established for them at Milltown Cannery. There were about 400 prisoners in the camp. The priest made an impression on them when they found he could speak German.

Like all Germans, they liked their songfests and he often led them in singing, as well as conducting religious services, for a large number of them were Catholics.

The war changed many things. Father Gordon missed the trips

to the reservations and other places to see his friends. He missed Paul but they kept up a steady correspondence all during the war years. The Chief's letters to Paul, some of which he has kept all these years, reveal much of what went on during those years.

On March 2, 1942, he wrote: "It is only 24 below this morning. Nice weather for the 2nd of March. . . .

"I have been planning to run down to Madison but the weather up here has been so severe that even driving is not pleasant. I had two funerals right in the midst of a big blizzard and below zero weather but my old body is still equal to the occasion even if I puff a little when I walk fast. I bet you I could still ride a camel!

"Paul, I am an old man but I have never really seen a winter like the present one. It got cold during the hunting season and never a thaw until last week when it thawed for two days a little and today 24 below and Spring just around the corner.

"By the way, I hope that opportunist Wendell W does not run again. He would not get to first base, I think, old Chief Blow Hard. I am almost in favor of another term for FDR. Let him die in office and Eleanor can take over, nes't pas? Infant terrible! Sepra gemon! (My French spelling is awful.)

"Visited with old Doc Meilicke last week. He is not in such good health but still carries on. Old Walter Lantz was taken to Madison General last week. Looks like cancer. Thus things go on sweetly and we await spring with anxiety. My C cards expire tomorrow but I expect another batch. Got 96 coupons last time. . . ."

Paul was busy with his Red Cross duties. Gas and tires were rationed and the priest felt more than he ever had the isolation of the parsonage at Long Lake. His aged father had gone back to Gordon and he was all alone. To get to Chicago, where Paul was stationed for a time, he had to drive to St. Paul and take a train. If he had a sick call at night, he had to put chains on his tires or have the county plow come in or get a team of horses to come in because the roads were either filled with snow or washed out, but he had to get there.

He wrote to Ke-Wah-Din (he always addressed Paul by his Indian name), "I am certainly alone here for the first time in years. I am getting used to cooking my own meals as I did years ago when I first hit this ranch. My dad is perfectly fine. I was up to see him last week. He is sitting pretty and contented. You might mail him a pipe if you happen to find one lying around loose and unclaimed. Just address Wm. Gordon, Gordon, Wis." Later that year, 1943, William Daniel Gordon died at the age of ninety-three.

Father Gordon was in Pittsburgh at the time and arrived home on the day of the funeral to hear of the death. He hurried to Gordon and arrived one hour before time for the funeral. He then officiated at the Requiem High Mass in the pioneer church erected by Anton Gordon, Philip Gordon's grandfather.

On May 16, 1942, Father Gordon wrote:
"Dear Ke-Wah-Din:

". . . Paul, I too was a little heart-sick when you wrote of so many things of the days gone by. . . .

"Tomorrow, Sunday, I will leave for Merrill. Fr. Rice has invited me down for two or three days. A new $100,000 school will be dedicated. This week, I was quite busy. On Monday, Bishop O'Connor dedicated the school at Reserve and I preached; Tuesday at Odanah, another new school dedicated and preached again. That evening we all went over to Bayfield for closing of 40 hours. The Bishop preached. Had a fine visit with him. He is as different from Bp. Reverman as I am from Shung Kai Check. He is a real good mixer, plain, common, friendly.

"I heard a week or two ago from John Daggett's mother that John is now in Newfoundland with a bunch of contractors, building air-bases. So that leaves St. Paul empty as far as I am concerned. . . . Hence my visits to St. Paul are always very hurried ones and back the same day. . . .

"Of course there is always this consolation — this situation will not be that way forever. This war is going to end sometime and I have a lousy idea that it will end this year — at least I am hoping so. . . .

"Paul, time is fleeting, eternity is long. It does seem only a few months ago since your good mother used to greet me. . . ." (The priest had read the Mass at her funeral.)

"I suppose you have lost all interest in politics for the duration. Stassen, Wilkie, Heil, and the rest of the guys. Same here since Floyd Olson died.

"Very little going on, Paul. Roads are not any too good yet. Besides Heil is not sending any State aid up here and people are complaining bitterly. But I always say, That's what you get for voting for a damn Republican."

Another unusual event happened in that year. Anyone reading the Congressional Record for June 11, 1943, will find Father Gordon offered the following opening prayer in the House of Representatives that day:

"Father Almighty, we lift our minds and hearts to Thee in sacred communion for these brief moments.

"We praise and adore Thee. We thank Thee for the evidences of Thy good will and love toward our people and our Nation.

"The black chimneys of industry and the glittering temples of commerce that dot our vast land all too well bespeak Thy favors and the afforded opportunity given to our great Nation to advance the welfare of its peoples.

"Let us, O good Lord, not forget that we need a faith in Thee reared like the giant cathedral deep and solid in the bosom of the earth. Grant us, we beseech Thee, a firm belief in Thy power and majesty, Thy justice and charity.

"Grant, we pray, that this legislative body be guided by true Christian principles, so that in the twilight of the lives of its individual Members well may it be said of them in the words of the ancient Latin hymn —

'Vexilla Regis prodeunt
'Fulget Crucis mysterium.'

"Bless, O Great Spirit, the Kitchi Manito of our forefathers, our Great White Father, our President and our Commander in Chief. Bless the Members of this Congress. Bless us all, dear Lord.

"We beg these favors of Thee in the name of the Most Holy Trinity — Father, Thee, and the Holy Ghost. Amen."

The Chief visited Paul whenever he could in Madison and in 1943 made a trip to Camp Grant where Paul was then Field Director of the Red Cross in charge of the camp office. The commanding general assembled Indians from all the different tribes to meet the Indian priest.

"Indians will win for the great chief in Washington," Father Gordon said. "More than 20,000 of the 320,000 Indians in the United States are serving in the nation's fighting forces."

As an example of the Indians' spirit and participation, he cited the town of Odanah on the Bad River Reservation which had a population of 700 and has sent 140 braves to the army and one young woman to the WAACs.

"My people are indeed proud to fight for Uncle Sam against the axis aggressors," Father Gordon was pleased to announce.

Whenever his ration cards would allow it, the Indian priest went back to keep up the old traditions — ricing, maple syrup making, hunting, fishing. He was now fifty-eight and he believed he had completely recovered from has malignancy. In 1943 he wrote, "Just a line or two as I wait to start out on my second day's hunt for the fleeting deer. I was to the Doc Olson cottage north of Grantsburg yesterday. Saw 23 does but not a single buck, so came home without the bacon. Going out west of here today on the St. Croix. Lots of deer out there is reported.

"Trust everything is going on well with thee. I have been unable to make the cities the past week. My gas was running low until the end of the week when our local board came through for almost 300 coupons. I am now pretty well fixed and will try to make use of some of them to get to the cities next week. . . .

"Dan wrote about a month ago. I sent the manuscript of the

book to them two months ago. Nothing about it from either of them. . . ."

The reference was to the book Dan Wallace was to have helped him with. The book apparently was never written but the "Outline for Biography of a Chippewa Indian Who Became a Catholic Priest" was published by the *Inter-County Leader* at Frederic, Wis. This is probably the manuscript referred to by Father Gordon.

Father Gordon seemed concerned about Paul's future, as the Red Cross was only for the duration. Many of his letters contained references to his future and advice about work, girls, etc. He seemed to think Paul deserved a promotion he never received. On April 20, 1944, he wrote:

". . . One does not always like to be doing good work but never moved to a better paying or higher or more responsible job. Just like in the army. First private, then corporal, sergeant, lieutenant, captain, major, colonel, general, etc., up and up and up, and more pay and more pay and more pay. Of course, you understand in my case all we priests get the same salary. The difference between a small parish and a big one is that there are more baptisms and more funerals and more marriages and as you know a priest gets a little fee for each performance. To state my case, last year (1943) I had two funerals and one marriage and perhaps 12 baptisms. . . .

"You have the satisfaction that you did and are doing a very good and even extraordinary work. . . . But as you wrote the work is only for the duration. Thereafter, you will take up other fields. Politics? Rather an uncertain and not always successful field. Witness poor Wendell Wilkie. Lot of headaches and lots of enemies and some friends. The Church? Well, lots of heartaches and requires too much advance preparation and you don't get much reward in this life. But it does give you a big kick out of life. I really do have the time of my life. There is not a day I do not laugh out loud to myself. The lumber business? It's a business career and mostly routine desk work and very few contacts except the office force and the meager social life of St. Paul. Your delight is to meet people and make contacts and visit places. You probably would be a little unhappy although your uncle Charley always seemed jovial and got a lot out of life and I imagine had many a good party, got great satisfaction out of doing good to Sisters and poor people. And he led a clean life. . . .

"Well, with me, I am now too old to look a long time ahead. Most of my life is behind me and your suggestion that I should rush work on my biography is a very sensible one. That is what I ought to do but you know how lazy one gets. Hardly any ambition. Nothing pushing you. Hence you delay and postpone and procrastinate ($64 word) and in the end do nothing except plan."

July 5, 1944, he wrote:

"Did you get my acceptance of the Bastille Day invite? I mailed a letter and the card from St. Joe's Hospital where I had my tonsils taken out which was almost as bad as the disease.

"Well, the old war seems to be coming to an end fast. What a blessing it will be for the whole world. I think we ought to plan a trip about 1946. By that time steamships will be back or maybe we will be able to fly over for about the same price."

Father Gordon spoke more and more of loneliness. On May 17, 1943 he wrote:

"Do you know, Ke-Wah-Din, as I grow older, I find it harder and harder to find people to associate with. Old friends die, go away. I am all alone again. Fr. Tabenicki who was with me (but miserable company) is now on his farm near Chetek, Wis., and my winter housekeeper is back near Hayward. Of course one gets used to anything.

"Right now I am trying to write my biography. So many have suggested it and Dan Wallace said he would edit and publish such a volume, but I worked for five hours yesterday and dashed off about 15 typewritten pages and I have not yet reached my 12th year in age. How many pages will it take when I reach my twentys and thirtys and fortys? It would take one book alone to tell of our Mediterranean trip and another to tell of my trip to Ireland and another of my schooling in Rome, in Innsbruck, in Washington, D. C., in St. Thomas, etc., etc."

When winter came he apparently was glad he did not have to eat his own cooking any longer. On November 20 he wrote:

". . . I have my winter housekeeper and janitor now with me and I can now get a mouthful of wild rice properly cooked with rabbit, squirrel, venison, or wild duck. . . ."

March 19, 1945, he wrote:

"I promised to help Fr. Fagan out in River Falls on Good Friday. He is not so well, so between us two old men we ought to go through the ritual without too many mistakes.

"Was in town last week but made no calls. Had forgotten my glasses at Father Guinney's, so drove down to pick them up, then called at Seven Corners for some Gingerale and then home. No place to go, Paul, and nobody to talk to there.

"It's a hell of a life for an old rounder like myself. But the war is bound to end someday and we can resume our old schedule. . . .

"I bet you, Paul, we will do a lot of running around when once the show is over. Just think of getting new cars, all the gas we need, all the tires we can use! And then cash in on our bonds.

"Drop us a line soon Paul. I had to give up my plans to go South. Tried three places to get a substitute priest but nothing doing. The manpower shortage has struck the clergy ranks and simply impossible to get help over a Sunday. . . ."

May 15, 1945:

"Arrived home safely and found things here O.K. Must have been a lot of love-making during my absence as I will have three marriages within the next week. . . .

"I'll take a couple of days off to visit around. Want to visit Dan and Ceil too. With all my fees coming from the marriages, I'll be in the velvet. . . .

"Sad news for our parish today. One of my boys reported

missing in action in Germany. Date May 1st. That is our first casualty and I feel bad, as I baptized the kid 20 years ago. He was Gene Murphy. Family all broken up. War is hell. . . ."

June 19, 1945:

". . . Dan Wallace and Ceil have moved back to the Ryan. We visited every night almost during my last week's stay there. . . .

"Before I was released from the hospital (June 7), had a steak dinner over at your aunt Jen's. . . . George is a nice old fellow. He came with his car to pick me up at the hospital and later brought me back. . . .

"I would like to get over to Reserve and Post. In fact, I have half a notion to run over there today and get a taste of venison. . . .

"I got a big kick out of your visit to the hospital while I was a prisoner there and especially that Mark Clark story about my Mass. I read Mass every Sunday for the soldiers and Mark Clark is a soldier. POSEYEMO. . . .

"Goodbye for the time being. Feeling fine since my release, but am taking it very easy. No more lawn mowing or wood chopping. POSEYEMO AND CHAPLAIN BASTILLE DAY VETERANS

CHAPTER
XX

Last Days of a Great Man

THE UNIQUE FRIENDSHIP BETWEEN THE CHIEF AND PAUL continued after the war. They knew each other intimately and understood each other in a way no one else did. Paul had heard Father Gordon's great oratory; but he had also been with him when he would drive for a half hour without saying a word, then apologize because he had been thinking.

He was with the Chief when he visited his mother or other relatives on the reservation and the only word he heard spoken was "Ba Zhu" (phonetic spelling, probably not a written word). A few gestures may have passed between them, a shake of the head, a smile, but when they left he knew that his aunt was all right, his mother's cousin was fine, everything was o.k.

In 1941 Father Gordon was in Chicago visiting Paul when he received the call that his mother, A-ta-ge-kwe, had died of pneumonia at the age of 86. She had gone back to the reservation many years ago and later lived in her little home in Gordon where Catherine Gordon McDonald now spends part of the summer. Catherine, who has a home in Superior, is a daughter of Father Gordon's brother Joe. She says, "This was his mother's house. She lived here until she died. She used to do all kinds of work, beadwork, tanning hides, she made jackets and sold them. People would bring their hides and she would tan them and make jackets. I don't know how she did it. She'd soak them and then scrape them. She was a beautiful sewer, knitter, she could do anything. The funny part of it was she never had to have glasses."

Father Gordon continued to visit the reservation as often as possible, keeping in touch with his remaining friends and relatives. But age and the ravages of his illness were taking their toll.

In 1946 after the war had ended, Paul spent a great deal of time visiting the Chief at his home at Long Lake. The priest would light a cigar — he loved to smoke cigars but couldn't learn to smoke a pipe — and was ready to discuss anything.

Paul said, "The only Catholic education I received was from my parents as a child, and from Father Gordon. On many occasions, whenever we discussed religion, if I had a question, he had the answer. He was an eloquent speaker on any subject. Certainly he was an authority on his own religion.

"We had different political views. He was a liberal and my family was always conservative. We spent long hours far into the night discussing politics and the merits of candidates. It had nothing to do with our friendship. This went on whether we were talking politics, religion, or history. He loved history and had an extensive library of Indian history.

"Father Gordon had an uncanny sense of humor. He saw a great deal of humor in things that other people didn't even think were funny. I think that's one of the reasons he and I got along so well. We laughed and got a big kick out of living."

In 1946 Father Gordon mentioned in a letter to Paul that maybe the war would be over and then they could travel again. But when Paul returned to Europe in 1947 the Chief was too ill to go. When Paul visited some of the countries they had traveled through twelve years earlier, many people remembered the Indian priest and his feathered headdress.

Paul's visit to Pope Pius XII was written up in Paul Light's column: ". . . Paul was informed by Vatican officials that the

Pope was in summer residence and was holding no audiences.

"Please get word to him," the St. Paul visitor said, "I came all the way from St. Paul to see him."

"It will do no good," he was told.

"Tell him I met him when he was in St. Paul as Cardinal Pacelli 11 years ago and that he invited me to see him if I ever came to Rome."

Paul was summoned for a private audience with the Pope who recalled that Paul's grandfather had restored a village church in the Vosges mountains of France after World War I. He asked many questions about the United States and expressed apprehension over the spread of Communism.

Father Gordon was in and out of the hospital from then on. He had planned to officiate at Paul's marriage in the chapel of St. Joseph's Hospital the latter part of November, but he was too sick.

After a long period in the hospital, November 6, 1946, to January 3, 1947, he wrote a letter for publication, thanking all his friends for their solicitude. He named a long list, including the Sisters of St. Joseph; Dr. William C. Carroll; Dr. Richard M. Leick; Dr. James V. Wilson; nurses and hospital personnel; the Most Reverend Archbishop of St. Paul; Governor and Mrs. Ed Thye; Dan and Ceil Wallace; Harry and Jen Carson; Monsignor Ed Casey; Fathers Peter Rice and Philip Krembs; Fathers Richard Doherty, James Guinney, and Francis Missia; school children from many places; and many, many others, including Paul, of course, who was a daily visitor.

"My debt to each and all can never be repaid. Left in our weak power is but to promise each a memento in my yet-to-be-read Holy Masses (may they be many) ere the twilight comes — prelude to the Great Adventure — 'and the evening comes, and the busy world is hushed, and the fever of life is over, and our work is done! Then in His mercy may He give us safe lodging and a holy rest, and peace at the last!' "

Paul recalls one of his visits at the hospital:

"I walked in one day and he had tears in his eyes. I asked him what happened. He said, 'The bishop was just here and he gave me the last rites of the church and I'm going to die and I'm happy about it!'

"I told him if I had a son I was going to call him Philip Gordon (Philip Gordon Villaume is living in St. Paul today).

"Father Gordon suffered a lot and was in and out of the hospital and it was hard on him. But the Sisters of St. Joseph's took good care of him."

Even during the intermittent periods out of the hospital, Father Gordon was still in there fighting, or at any rate, lending his support to others taking up the cause. On January 4, he appeared in a picture with others, although he was evidently a very sick man. More than 100 Chippewa Indians had joined the Inter Tribal Organization to outline their claims for approximately 223 million dollars which they say is due them for their original lands."

On May 2, 1948, Paul drove the Chief home to St. Patrick's for the last time. He was home a few weeks when he called to tell Paul that he had to return to the hospital. But somehow he attended Bastille Day on July 14. He arrived in a wheel chair. It was his last public appearance.

Paul spent the evening of September 30 with the priest and left at midnight.

"I received a call the following morning, October 1, 1948, telling me that Father Gordon was dying. Ten minutes later I was in the room and I had the privilege of joining the nuns in final prayer. The nuns tell me that he recognized my voice. He died peacefully soon after."

Although he never received world-wide acclaim, Father Gordon had put up a good fight for human rights and the causes he believed in. The first Indian priest in the United States was loved by all who knew him. They loved him because he loved everyone. They loved him because of his broad-minded, ecumenical views. They respected him for his struggle for rights of the Indians, the farmers, and anyone else whose rights were being violated; for his love of children; for his magic oratory.

Father Gordon was a man ahead of his time. If he were alive today, he would be disappointed that the cause he fought for is still not resolved. He would, no doubt, still be in there fighting. He was truly a man of two worlds — the white and the Indian, as well as the worldly and the spiritual.

TI-BISH-KO-GI-JIK, the first American Indian in the country to become a priest, was honored in 1972 when a new Knights of Columbus Council was established, comprising a number of area parishes, including St. Patrick's, Centuria. The unanimous choice of a name was "Father Philip Gordon Council 6370 of the Knights of Columbus."

GENEALOGICAL TABLE

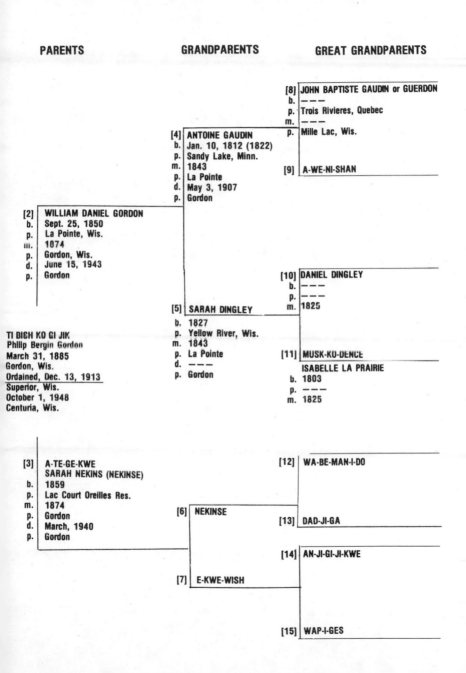

PARENTS

GRANDPARENTS

GREAT GRANDPARENTS

[8] JOHN BAPTISTE GAUDIN or GUERDON
b. — — —
p. Trois Rivieres, Quebec
m. — — —
p. Mille Lac, Wis.

[4] ANTOINE GAUDIN
b. Jan. 10, 1812 (1822)
p. Sandy Lake, Minn.
m. 1843
p. La Pointe
d. May 3, 1907
p. Gordon

[9] A-WE-NI-SHAN

[2] WILLIAM DANIEL GORDON
b. Sept. 25, 1850
p. La Pointe, Wis.
m. 1874
p. Gordon, Wis.
d. June 15, 1943
p. Gordon

[10] DANIEL DINGLEY
b. — — —
p. — — —
m. 1825

[5] SARAH DINGLEY
b. 1827
p. Yellow River, Wis.
m. 1843
p. La Pointe
d. — — —
p. Gordon

[11] MUSK-KU-DENCE
ISABELLE LA PRAIRIE
b. 1803
p. — — —
m. 1825

TI BISH KO GI JIK
Philip Bergin Gordon
March 31, 1885
Gordon, Wis.
Ordained, Dec. 13, 1913
Superior, Wis.
October 1, 1948
Centuria, Wis.

[3] A-TE-GE-KWE
SARAH NEKINS (NEKINSE)
b. 1859
p. Lac Court Oreilles Res.
m. 1874
p. Gordon
d. March, 1940
p. Gordon

[12] WA-BE-MAN-I-DO

[6] NEKINSE

[13] DAD-JI-GA

[14] AN-JI-GI-JI-KWE

[7] E-KWE-WISH

[15] WAP-I-GES

NOTE: The following abbreviations are used in this table = b. (born), m. (married), d. (died), p. (place).

SOURCES OF INFORMATION

~~~~~~

Numerous sources were used in research work for this book, some for authentic facts and some just for background. Many people have been helpful.

The manuscript entitled "Outline for Biography of a Chippewa Indian Priest," loaned by the Chancery Office of the Superior Diocese, formed a guideline for the arrangement of the book. It is not entirely clear who wrote the outline, but it appears to me it was written by Father Gordon at the instigation of Fred Holmes and Dan Wallace, who planned to write a book about the priest. This book was never written. According to Paul Villaume, the men were all just too old to do the work.

Reverend Raymond L. Schoone of the Chancery Office, Superior, also furnished copies of correspondence between Father Gordon and church officials.

Much information was derived from Father Gordon's series in the *Inter-County Leader,* published by the Inter-County Publishing Association, at Frederic, Wis. Bernice Abrahamzon, who is employed there, was indispensable in arranging time and making the files available to me.

Other sources of information and background were the following:

Hand-written notes of Father Gordon (from Orrin McGrath).

"Gordon and the Gordon Family," an article written by Eldon Marple, Haywood.

"Antoine Gordon," a biographical sketch in *Upper Lakes Region Commemorative Record.*

Heirship approval, estate of Antoine Gordon.

Various church and ancestry records — Gordon, Bayfield, Long Lake, Reserve. Some of these supplied by Trudy Wolf, Stone Lake, and Orrin McGrath, North Fond du Lac, Wis.

Interviews with people who knew Father Gordon:

Paul Villaume.

Catherine Gordon McDonald.

Mrs. Marie Mulvaney Hersant.

Louis de Angelo.

Edith Anderson.

O. D. and Mrs. McGrath.

Mrs. Joe Rogers.

Charlie Turner.

Katie Gohke.

Scipio Wise.

Charlie Coons.

Mr. and Mrs. Lawrence Reidner.

Sinon Lynch.

Benny Isham.

Russell H. Johnson.

Others who gave information:

Tony Wise.

Warren Kirk.

Trudy Wolf (Mrs. Burt Wolf).

The following libraries and librarians:

Mary Ellen Braafaldt, Reference Librarian, Duluth Public Library.

Mrs. Barbara Knotts, Superior Public Library.

Carol Martinson, Reference Librarian, St. Paul Public Library.

Minnesota Historical Library.

Mrs. Leona Ryan, Archives Librarian, College of St. Thomas.

Thomas R. Sykora and Captain H.C. Inches of the Great Lakes Historical Library.

The following published books:

Badger History.

Cadot Family Stories.

Centennial History of Gordon (sent to me by John Love).

Curtis, Natalie, *The Indian Book.*

Densmore, Frances, *How Indians Use Wild Plants for Food.*

Dictionary of Wisconsin History.

Gridley, Marion E., *Indians of Today.*

Habig, Marion A., *Heralds of the King: The Franciscans of the St. Louis-Chicago Province, 1858-1958* (furnished by Franciscan Herald Press).

History of the Catholic Church in America.

History of the Great Lakes.

Hoar, Col. W. G., *History Is Our Heritage.*

Kellogg, Louise Phelps, *Rise and Fall of Old Superior.*

Kinney, J. P., *Indian Forest and Range.*

Purcell, William Gray, *St. Croix Trail Country.*

Ritzenthaler, Robert E. and Pat, *The Woodland Indians of the Western Great Lakes.*

Stewart, Lillian Kimball, *A Pioneer of Old Superior.*

The Wisconsin Magazine.

Wisconsin Magazine of History.

The Wisconsin Story.

Clippings from various publications:

American Legion Magazine.

Minneapolis *Times.*

St. Paul *Dispatch* — St. Paul *Pioneer Press.*

St. Paul *Daily News.*

Superior *Evening Telegram.*